"Do you feel the need for a change in your life—a new job, a new purpose? Don't let fear hold you back. You too can find the courage to change with the wisdom collected by Kate Swoboda in this helpful, cheerful, and delightfully readable book."

> —**Daniel H. Pink**, *New York Times* bestselling author of *Drive* and *A Whole New Mind*

"*The Courage Habit* combines the latest research into what creates genuine change with the spiritual view that fear is a gateway to fearlessness. Drawing on her experience coaching clients, personal stories, doable (non-silly) exercises, and her ever-present warmth, this book teaches you the four key habits to face what is holding you back and live your most courageous life."

> —**Susan Piver**, bestselling author of *Start Here Now*

"If there's anything I've learned and taken to heart in the last few years, it's that we only have one life to live and we could all stand to spend more time on what makes us happy and less time feeling like we're about to implode from anxiety, shame, guilt, and fear. *The Courage Habit* is a great reminder that *you* control your destiny, and *you* have the power to make changes from the inside out to have the life you want, need, and deserve."

> —**Sarah Knight**, *New York Times* bestselling author of *The Life-Changing Magic of Not Giving a F*ck* and *Get Your Sh*t Together*

D0057684

"Anyone that's completed a half-Ironman knows a thing or two about courage and emotional resilience. In her new book, *The Courage Habit*, Kate Swoboda discusses the connection between psychological daring and habit formation, and explains how to unlock your hidden potential to reach lofty goals. Essential reading, whether you're planning on tackling an Ironman or more courageously tackling the challenges and opportunities of life."

> —**Dean Karnazes**, ultramarathoner and *New York Times* bestselling author

"By challenging the reader to face and embrace fear, *The Courage Habit* provides us with a clear path to self-acceptance and emotional freedom. *The Courage Habit* provides a real-life road map for anyone seeking to face and release their fears. It's a powerful invitation that challenges us all to step into radical self-acceptance and emotional freedom."

> —**Rich and Yvonne Dutra-St.John**, *Oprah* guests, and cofounders of Challenge Day and the Be the Change Movement

"This book is the perfect blend of 'I've been there too' personal stories from Kate, inspiring client stories, and evidence-based strategy to not only just 'feel more courageous,' but to turn courage into a daily habit for you. What a refreshing, practical, smart take on a much-needed quality that each of us needs to live a meaningful life!"

> —**Kate Northrup**, author of *Money*, and creator of Origin

"*The Courage Habit* is a definitive guide to your new understanding of fear and courage, and what they really are, and how they can both be reshaped to support the life you actually want to live. *The Courage Habit* will help you to stop trying to be 'fearless,' and start creating something deeper and richer for your life: living from a place of courage. And what that will produce for your life is truly revelatory."

—**SARK**, author, artist, inspirationist, www.planetsark.com

"Open this book and find the insights and tools to work with your fear in an entirely new way. Being afraid is part of being human, but with Kate's well-researched and client-tested guidance, that's no longer bad news. With this book in hand, you will be able to choose much more often to do and create what you most desire. Allow Kate's wise guidance to shine light wherever fear has you crimped and doubting. And then celebrate the heck out of what happens."

—**Jennifer Louden**, author of *The Woman's Comfort Book* and *The Life Organizer*

"Stop running on autopilot and start living the authentic, fulfilling life you've been yearning for with *The Courage Habit*. Kate Swoboda's practical tools based on scientific research will teach you how to work with your fears, tap into your deepest desires, and build the skills to make your big visions real. Through her vulnerable truth-telling and compassionate curiosity, Kate models *The Courage Habit*, and you'll feel like she's right there in your corner as you take each courageous step forward."

—**Jennifer Lee**, author of *The Right-Brain Business Plan*

"Pretty much everyone in the world needs more courage, so pretty much everyone needs *The Courage Habit* on their bedside table. Whether you're trying to drum up enough courage to negotiate for more paid vacation time at work or trying to muster up the courage to publish your first blog post, the guidance in this book will help."

—**Alexandra Franzen**, author of *50 Ways to Say You're Awesome* and *You're Going to Survive*

"In self-help today, the term 'fearless' has taken wings and can make people feel like they're 'doing it wrong' if they still experience fear. Kate so gracefully and clearly tells the reader how to work with fear, pinpoint our fear-based stories to reframe them, and live their most courageous life. Every chapter in this book is a gem!"

—**Andrea Owen**, author of *52 Ways to Live a Kick-Ass Life* and *How to Stop Feeling Like Sh*t*

"We treat fear as a thing to either be ashamed of or to crush. 'Kate Courageous' helps us understand it is an essential, and survivable, part of doing great work in the world."

—**Pamela Slim**, author of *Body of Work* and *Escape from Cubicle Nation*

BLOGGERS

"Fear and doubt will always be part of the journey, because as humans we'll always encounter fear and doubt. *The Courage Habit* will IGNITE your courage and have you extinguishing the negative voices in your head. You are on the path to greatness, so allow *The Courage Habit* to light the way!"

—**John Lee Dumas**, *Entrepreneur on Fire*

"In Kate Swoboda's *The Courage Habit*, she illuminates what so many of us are seeking: a practical, attainable path out of our fear-driven actions and into a life created by courage. Kate's book speaks both as a seasoned fellow traveler and an expert with an invaluable depth of knowledge in the supporting sciences. This is the book for all of us looking at the gap between where we are and where we want to be, but are afraid to go."

—**Rachel W. Cole**, coach and teacher at www.rachelwcole.com

"Warning/threat/promise: After working through the four steps laid out for you in *The Courage Habit*, you won't have any excuses for not reaching your Big Goals or Scary Dreams. Get ready to bust through the negative patterns and stories that are holding you back, in a totally grounded and accessible way. Kate Swoboda gives you the toolbox to live your most courageous life."

—**Michelle Ward**, *When I Grow Up Coach*

"This book is a huge exhale! Not only does it normalize the fear that we all live with, but teaches us how to *move toward our fear* with love and compassion. Once we are working with our fear instead of fighting against it (or pretending it doesn't exist), Kate teaches us how to create habits around courage that allow us to create what we truly want in our lives. This book is wise, practical, and full of compassion."

—**Andrea Scher**, *Superhero Life*

"Like the friend who always sees through your B.S. and can tell what's *really* going on with you, *The Courage Habit* will make you feel relieved, safe, and hopeful as you face your fears, and the where-the-rubber-meets-the-road practices will help you change the habits that are holding you back."

—**Laura Simms**, founder of *Your Career Homecoming*

"It's one thing to talk about cultivating courage. It's an altogether different thing to illuminate exactly how to be resilient when fear emerges, which is exactly what Kate Swoboda has done in *The Courage Habit*. Pairing research-backed steps with her extensive experiences as a coach and founder of a renowned coach training program, Kate Swoboda shows readers how to make courage a 'routine' you default to—so that you can move through discomfort and obstacles, and live, work, and play from a place of wholeness and unapologetic self-acceptance. *The Courage Habit* has sharpened my skill set as a coach. I love everything about this book— and you will too!"

—**Alexia Vernon**, author of *Step into Your Moxie*

"Kate takes the adage, 'Feel the fear and do it anyway!' from rally cry to process—giving us practical tools to recognize our own fear patterns and to choose courageous responses. *The Courage Habit* is a modern day how-to manual, taking us from self-sabotaging our dreams to moving forward with resilience and self-compassion. It's a must-read for any woman who feels like fear is holding her back from claiming her true potential in the world!"

—**Molly Mahar**, founder of Stratejoy

"Through *The Courage Habit*, Kate 'Courageous' Swoboda lets the world know exactly how to dance with fear—and it is a dance. Like anything in life, we must learn to move, flow, and act with the fear that is present. *The Courage Habit* is informative, practical, compassionate, and both life-changing and world-changing."

—**Julie Daley**, *Unabashedly Female*

The Courage Habit

How to accept your fears, release the past, and **live your courageous life**

KATE SWOBODA

New Harbinger Publications, Inc.

Publisher's Note

This publication is designed to provide accurate and authoritative information in regard to the subject matter covered. It is sold with the understanding that the publisher is not engaged in rendering psychological, financial, legal, or other professional services. If expert assistance or counseling is needed, the services of a competent professional should be sought.

Distributed in Canada by Raincoast Books

Copyright © 2018 by Kate Swoboda

New Harbinger Publicatio ns, Inc.
5674 Shattuck Avenue
Oakland, CA 94609
www.newharbinger.com

The Courage Habit is a registered trademark. We claim this trademark even when the ® symbol is not displayed.

Cover design by Amy Shoup

Acquired by Camille Hayes

Edited by Erin Raber

All Rights Reserved

Library of Congress Cataloging-in-Publication Data on file

20	19	18								
10	9	8	7	6	5	4	3	2	1	First Printing

Contents

Foreword

In a long and deep life, we will have to find our courage. We will have many moments when, as this lovely book encourages, we *feel* our fear yet dive in anyway, only to emerge transformed. One of the most transformational events in my own life followed this pattern to a tee. In 1998, when I tore open my first student loan bill, I was terrified. I stared at it for a solid minute, blinking and dumbstruck. How on earth could I afford *that much*, every single month?

I had just completed my masters in somatic psychology, and adored how this field allowed me to share my gifts. But my wonderful degree program hadn't breached the taboo of money or instructed us on how to turn our training into a profitable career. As a fiercely nontraditional kind of gal, I knew I wouldn't feel at home in the corporate world. Yet I had no clue what other career options existed, let alone how I could earn the kind of money to cover that monthly student loan bill and enjoy a comfortable lifestyle.

I had no idea how to solve this conundrum. I panicked. I gave serious thought to packing a bag, skipping the country, and finishing my days as a quirky, globetrotting vagabond on the run from the banks. Thankfully, I made a different choice. I took a deep breath, slowed down, and felt all my shame and fear. I needed to face this riddle head-on: How could I create a career I loved, share my gifts, and pay my bills?

I couldn't see the answer to that riddle when I asked it. I simply trusted that I could create something new, even if I couldn't see what it was yet. As Kate Swoboda so beautifully defines courage, I was "willing to follow an unknown path." The book you hold in your hands has helped me understand moments of courage like that in a deeper way and has also gifted me with the tools and inspiration to choose more of them.

Courage can be epic and life changing, but we can also call upon it in subtle moments too. Each time we choose a smidgen more awareness, honesty, or compassion, we are brave. Getting vulnerable is brave. And, sometimes, merely asking ourselves what we *really* want takes super-heroic guts.

So, why do we sometimes step boldly into our courageous choices, and other times slink (or sprint) away? Kate gives the most empowering explanation possible: it's a matter of practice. Courage is a *habit*, she argues. It's a muscle we can strengthen for each small or big victory at a time. That means that anyone with a little patience and guidance can practice the Courage Habit... and get better and better at it.

This endeavor must be a gentle one, though. We can't shame ourselves into sustainable change, and the "tough love" approach simply doesn't work for emotional healing. I needed all the gentleness I could muster as I walked my "unknown path" after that student-loan-bill crossroads. Dealing with money and career brought me to deep inner work around my value, empowerment, and safety. Step by step, I found my own style of creative entrepreneurship and began applying my gifts and training to guide others in their own journeys with money and much more.

Today, in my work as a financial therapist, I have the great delight of witnessing my community members make courageous choices every day. I applaud them for summoning the courage to peek at their credit scores (when it scares the living broccoli out of them) and encourage minidance parties when they have that tough money conversation with their sweeties. I remind them over and over again how *brave* it is to change old patterns, make bold, new choices, and do it all with love and panache.

Heroic journeys like these—and like the one you're on, dear reader—require more than logic and blueprints. Deep, meaningful transformation requires rationality *and* emotional intelligence; heart *and* grit. These are the precisely elements you'll find in this book.

If it took courage for you to even pick up this book, take heart. Kate won't wag a disciplinarian's finger at you, barking at you to overcome fear through sheer willpower. Instead, she will reassure you: Fear is a universal experience and not a cause for shaming yourself. (Whew.) She'll help you do the improbable and miraculous: make *friends* with fear. And, she will coax you into honoring that soft, vulnerable voice of hope within you by taking courageous action toward creating the life you truly want.

These pages are brimming with inspiration, helpful strategies, and a whole lot of warmth. This book isn't superficial or motivational fluff; it's imminently practical and full of heart, just like Kate.

I'm so happy we now have Kate's beautiful book to guide us through all the micro- and mega-moments in our lives that call for gumption and grit. May we all gently and mindfully stretch a little farther into our growing edges. May loving awareness be our refuge and lodestar. May we all take this book's message to heart, and let it inspire us to live fuller, richer, more authentic lives one courageous choice at a time.

—Bari Tessler
financial therapist
author of *The Art of Money*
http://www.BariTessler.com

Introduction

Here's the thing about the day when you officially decide that you've got to change your life: you don't even see it coming. When that day arrived for me, it was an ordinary, cold San Francisco morning in December that started like any other. I got up that morning, hating the sound of my alarm clock. I got dressed, hating the feel of the stiff, button-down shirt and tailored suit. I got into my car, hating the commute that was ahead of me. There was only one thing that I was looking forward to: as soon as my workday was done, and I attended a meeting that had cruelly been scheduled for the last hour of the last day before Christmas vacation, I could go home and not think about work for two whole weeks.

Later that afternoon, sitting in that meeting while two of my colleagues debated whether we should all spend part of our Christmas vacations outlining plans for a new project, my mind wandered, and that's when the truth asserted itself: *I don't want to do this, anymore.*

I've always been a person who prefers pragmatism over drama. I've had very few moments that would qualify as "earth shattering," but this was one of them. With that thought, I felt dizzy in my chair as I recognized how very real this truth was, even as much as it surprised me. *I didn't want to do this, anymore—since when?* I had seriously hustled to get this job, hustled for years to prove myself to veteran colleagues, and hustled every paycheck down to its last dime to pay my student loans and buy those stiff suits. I had volunteered extra hours and signed up for extra committees, and people on the hiring team had quietly taken me aside to let me know that if I applied for an upcoming promotional position, I'd be a shoo-in.

I had told myself and everyone else so many times that this lifestyle was what I wanted. Here I was, lucky enough to be the woman who got what she'd worked for. My entire overachieving life had lead me here. And now, after all that work, I was thinking the one thing that made no sense to think: *I don't want to do this, anymore.*

This truth was an inconvenient fact that followed me throughout Christmas vacation even if I tried to ignore it. *I didn't want to do this, anymore.* I didn't want the job or the suits, even if they came with clout. I didn't want to spend my Christmas break outlining a new project, all so that I could impress colleagues who mostly bickered with one another and set up power plays. I didn't want this to still be my life a year from now and the year after that.

I had felt the call to change my life for a while, and I had been pushing that truth away for a long time because that call always came with a healthy dose of fear. I had responded to my fear by doing whatever I could to make it go away. I would work ever harder to distract myself from my feelings that *something just wasn't right.* I had focused on taking on extra work, so that I'd gain external validation from bosses and colleagues. But, behind the scenes, I regularly had headaches, body aches, and exhaustion. My moods frequently alternated between irritated or depressed, which I hid behind smiles, nods, and reassurances that everything was fine. To make myself feel better, I got little highs off being busy and the praise that came from colleagues who remarked upon how hard I worked. The problem was, the highs were harder to come by and didn't last for as long, and the distractions were no longer as effective at masking how I truly felt inside. The truth—*I don't want to do this, anymore*—had become too hard to ignore.

I spent most of that Christmas break vacillating between hiding out in a haze of television and what I call "desperate journaling." (You know, the kind of journaling where you keep trying to answer the rather intimidating question, "If you had a million dollars and all the time in the world, what would you do with your life?") Somewhere between journal prompts and reality television, I identified the uncomfortable sensation in my body, and realized with some surprise: *That feeling is fear. I know things need to change, but I'm completely afraid of actually changing them.*

I was so used to hustling to make sure that I appeared confident and put-together to the outside world that I hadn't realized how fear was calling the shots in every area of my life. I was the poster child for rocking a to-do list and looking courageous on the outside, while perpetually feeling like I wasn't good enough on the inside. But, I could no longer ignore the fact that this way of living wasn't working.

As I tuned in to what I was feeling instead of pushing it away, I noticed that deep down I was afraid of…everything. It wasn't just about the job. Sure, I was afraid of being unhappy if I stayed and was intimidated by the thought of switching careers, but this ran deeper. I was afraid that I'd never figure out who I was or what I wanted. I berated myself for being so confused and for not having immediate answers. Since none of my friends, family, or colleagues had ever talked about feeling the same confusion I was experiencing, I thought that I was alone in it. I was afraid of being judged if I started talking about what felt true or if I made choices that were different than what others expected. Lacking a plan, I did what felt necessary in that moment. Instead of pushing away the fear, I did something I had never done before: I acknowledged that the fear existed and that it had controlled me without my realizing it. *Okay, so, I'm afraid,* I remember thinking, turning the idea over and over. Now with more awareness of the situation, I had another realization: *I had a choice.* I could go back to pushing away the fear, which would keep me exactly where I had been, or I could start dealing with my fears differently, in ways that required courage but that might result in the authentic happiness that I'd been searching for.

For several months thereafter, I was resolved. At first, I thought that simply "putting my mind to it" and deciding to face my fear would be enough. All I needed to do was tell my self-doubt to take a hike, and then I could start living the life of my dreams, right? But the months that followed brought near-constant stops and starts as the old patterns didn't go away so easily. I was constantly taking one step forward and then one step back. There were weeks I'd find the courage within myself to speak up even if my opinion was unpopular. Or I'd come home and skip the extra workload in favor of writing fiction, another thing I had abandoned around the time that I started trying to climb a career ladder.

Then, there were other weeks, when I found myself feeling more insecure and uncertain about where my future was headed. During those weeks, I'd find myself agreeing—yet again—to take on more committee work for colleagues, just to get a little hit of their approval. I didn't understand how I could know so deeply that something needed to be different, yet find it so difficult to take the action required to do things differently. This wasn't how it happened in the movies, on television, or in any inspirational book I'd ever read.

At first, all I could manage was to just keep coming back to what I knew was true: *I don't want to do this, anymore.* I kept asking myself what I really wanted instead. I decided to let the answers that came up when I asked that question just be what they were, even though initially I judged them as being either too vanilla or totally unrealistic. *I want to write. I want to spend a summer in Italy learning Italian. I want to work with people in some way that makes their lives better. I want to teach.*

Today, in hindsight, I can speak more clearly to what I was coming to understand during that pivotal time of searching and uncertainty. First, discontent and unhappiness are signals worth listening to. There's an authentic part of all of us that refuses to be a liar and pretend that things are okay even when they really are not. This part of us will keep showing up through feelings like exhaustion, resentment, numbing out, or joylessness. Not feeling great about your life? Stop seeing those feelings as problems to quickly be rid of, and instead pay attention to *why* those feelings are showing up in the first place.

Second, our desires are valid. What we want for our lives *matters*, whether the things we want are simplistic or audacious. Our personal ambitions aren't selfish, and often, we only have a capacity for truly giving to or supporting others when our own inner well is full. Our desires are worthy of our attention and deserve to be a primary focus in our lives.

Third, going after what we desire will always involve some sort of fear or self-doubt. There's no way around that. There is no one who is perfectly "fearless." This person doesn't exist. Going after what you truly want will require coming back, again and again, to owning and understanding your fears. We can't just brush the fear to the side and make a to-do list. We've got to examine our fear responses, and work with and through those responses.

Finally, change isn't as simple as "deciding that things will be different." We all have patterned, habit-driven aspects to the ways we think and how we act. If we want to make bold, courageous life changes, we need to also understand how our habitual ways of being are either supporting or stopping us from change. Our ingrained habits influence the actions that we do or don't take.

If you see clearly how fear and habit-formation affect our behavior during times of change, the path to true life change becomes more obvious: We respond to fear in habitual ways, and far more predictably than we might initially realize, which means that seeing the routines that we default to during times of stress, challenges, or change is crucial. Understanding the role of fear in habitual routines, breaking them down, and creating different, courageous habits is how you change your life.

That difficult Christmas happened more than a decade ago, and today life looks radically different. After studying my own fear-based responses and the behavioral change factors that underlie our quests to lead better lives, I became a life coach working one-on-one with clients who, like me, wanted to shift something about their lives but they weren't sure how. With time, the scope of my practice narrowed to focus specifically on working with how we experience fear and practice courage. Later, I moved from working with individuals to facilitating retreats, workshops, programs, and seminars. As I've listened to thousands of hours of client stories and poured through research on behavior science and neuropsychology, I've learned some critical things about human behavior and how fear operates when we're trying to change.

We all know what it feels like to want something more for our lives, yet hesitate to act because fear or self-doubt looms large. It doesn't matter what the desire is, how big or small the change might seem, our fear routines are where we get stuck. So, changing those fear routines is the heart of where we get unstuck. This process of getting unstuck through authentic self-examination and releasing old habits, rather than doggedly trying to white-knuckle your way through fear, requires incredible courage. And, make no mistake: Courage absolutely can be cultivated. Courage isn't something you're born with; it's a specific set of strategies you can learn and choose to practice until a courageous way of being becomes your habitual way of being.

When I'm standing in front of a room full of workshop attendees or running an online course, at some point I'll survey the crowd by asking, "So what is it that you truly and deeply want to be different in your life?" Some people want to do something tangible and goal oriented, while others want to shift a way of being. Here are just a few of the things that people have told me when asked what they want to be different in their lives:

More time, more money, more sex.

Have more fun.

To give perfectionism the boot.

Make decisions with confidence, without doubting myself, or second-guessing myself.

Just be myself; be happy with who I am; feel like I'm enough.

Feel like I'm totally capable and can create what I want in my life.

Less insecurity.

To feel more confident and capable when making decisions.

Writing that book.

Improving my marriage.

Stop comparing myself and feeling like other people are prettier, more successful, or thinner.

Lose the weight.

I want to accept myself so that I don't feel like anything needs to be different.

Better boundaries with people who criticize me. I want to stop caring what they think.

I want to change jobs.

Get focused and finish what I start.

What all these participants are talking about is the desire to marry the inner and the outer, which is at the root of what we all crave. To match who we are on the inside (our values, deepest desires, and creative expression) with how we live day-to-day is what creates personal happiness and fulfillment. We want to be the people we feel we're meant to be. We want to be ourselves, and trust that that's enough.

However, when asking those same people a follow-up question about what has stopped them from making that change, they can give me a thousand different reasons for why change hasn't happened: there's not enough time or money; they're stuck because of how they were raised; it's the fault of that shitty ex-husband, a health challenge, or a crappy boss. Most reasons are a cover for the same thing: being afraid. They might call it something different, like self-doubt, but really we're talking about fear.

When we don't follow up on our desires for change with action, an old, habituated fear routine has taken over without us realizing it or being aware of it. It starts simply enough: You decide you want to do something differently, such as write the book you know you have in you or communicate better with a partner. Then, something goes awry. It might not have seemed like you were "afraid" when you ditched your book-writing goals for Facebook, or in that white-hot moment of anger at your partner when you offered potshots instead of speaking respectfully. In the moment, you might have had plenty of logical justifications for why you told yourself you'd change, and didn't.

Trying to navigate a new way of behaving is stressful, and stress is synonymous with fear. The brain is an intelligent organism that will seek the fastest, most efficient way to relief when confronted with stress. To lessen stress, the brain begins throwing out impulses based on what has worked for stress relief in the past. Some people feel impulses to procrastinate in response to feelings of self-doubt, while others do what I did and strive to be perfect and hustle to overachieve. When the brain is confronted with the challenge of trying to choose new behavior, the older and more familiar behaviors are the much less stressful option. This is precisely why change is so difficult. Try to take a new step such as moving in the direction of something you've long dreamed of doing, and your brain will flood you with anxiety because this is new and unfamiliar. If you ditch the plan to go after the dream and instead choose what's known and therefore safe, you'll be rewarded as the brain relaxes. Your brain likes predictability, and it's primed to "reward" you for choosing the familiar responses and routines.

Whether you're contemplating making a bold move and feeling paralyzed around taking the first step, or if you're trying to make changes and finding that you can't stick with them, these impulses of fear, anxiety, or discomfort are all part of your body's biochemical desires to keep life comfortable through continuity. Instead of seeing these feelings as a sign that the change you desire isn't really for you, understand that these are normal feelings in response to change, a sort of ingrained self-protection mechanism.

Here's the good news: If you understand how fear works on this level of the brain, you can recognize what the impulses are and start "retraining" the brain by teaching it that there are other ways to respond instead of the fear-based impulses that you're used to. Cultivating courageous behaviors as a regular part of your day and as a response to feelings of fear can stop fears from getting in the way of creating a bolder, more courageous life. When courage becomes a habit, it's easier to take action in the direction of the changes you desire.

Instead of letting the same fear patterns run seemingly outside of your control, you can look at each piece of the pattern, get honest and real about how you typically respond to fear, and make conscious, deliberate choices to respond differently and courageously. Armed with a better understanding of the brain's impulses, and of how to make behavioral changes through habit-formation, you can release old fear patterns and live your courageous life by practicing what I call the "Courage Habit."

Breaking Down the Courage Habit

This book will follow the coaching model, asking you to clarify what you want and how fear has kept you from getting it, and then showing you how you can use the Courage Habit process to work with your fears differently, this time. Working in real time with a coaching client, we typically meet for biweekly phone sessions for at least three months, with the client using the time between sessions for integrating and implementing the changes we talk about during our sessions. We start our coaching work by defining a Primary Focus and getting a sense of this most courageous self that the client wants to emerge.

In Chapter 1, we'll talk about what it is that you want to create in your life, what goals you've shied away from, or what ways of being you've found it difficult to change. What big dreams have you been holding back? If your "most courageous self" was the one running the show, what would you be doing differently? We'll get real about your truest, most authentic desires for your life.

In Chapter 2, things get exciting as you get some education on habit-formation—the keys to unlocking behavior change. Habits run on a cue-routine-reward loop in the brain, which I'll break down in detail in the chapter. Understanding this loop will help you to stop responding to fear and self-doubt in the same ways, so that new change is possible. Instead of playing out a fear-based cue-routine-reward loop, you'll be learning a more effective alternative. When you feel fear, you'll learn how to create the four parts of the Courage Habit as your new "routine." This will get you the "reward" that you desire, and allow you to go after the life you really want with more resilience and less self-doubt, fear, or hesitation.

The four parts of the Courage Habit that you'll learn in Chapters 3 to 6 are all research-backed steps that give you more resilience in the face of fear. Imagine that! Instead of fear being this feeling that stops you, or that you have to fight against, you can *choose* behaviors that will leave you more resilient and grounded, even when doubts arise. You won't be getting rid of the fear, but you'll stop getting stuck in the fear. As you start practicing these steps, you'll start to feel like you're truly capable of creating the life that you want.

Each chapter will be devoted to breaking down each part of the process. Here's an overview of the four parts:

- Access the body.

- Listen without attachment.

- Reframe limiting Stories.

- Reach out and create community.

Access the body. Fear isn't logical; we feel it in our bodies before we can "reason with" the voices of doubt or inner criticism. That's why we start by accessing the body, so that you'll be able to recognize fear sensations in the body right when they start but before they can overwhelm you. Accessing the body is a powerful tool for counteracting feelings of self-doubt that arise. Research published in the American Journal of Psychiatry clearly shows that mindfulness-based interventions alleviate stress and anxiety, something that's critical when making big life changes (Kabat-Zinn et al. 1992). You'll be slowing down and getting mindful to get smarter about how your fear is operating and what you can do to keep it from running you.

Listen without attachment. Most of us want to avoid dealing with any fears or critical voices within. It's one of the ways that we try to outrun fear. The multiple Internet memes about kicking fear's ass are a clear indication that our culture is constantly reinforcing our desire to get rid of fear. When we do tune in to any voices of self-doubt or criticism, most conventional advice is to shout those voices into submission. How well has that worked for you in the past? Do the voices always seem to come back? When you learn to listen without attachment, you'll be taking radically different action with that Inner Critic. Instead of trying to fight against or ignore the Critic, you'll create a relationship with it that's based in respectful communication and setting boundaries. Over time, you'll find that this often angry or belittling voice of judgment isn't as intimidating as you'd thought.

Reframe limiting Stories. Once you've slowed down enough to recognize the fear cues through accessing the body and you're listening to fear without attachment, you're ready to shift out of "I can't" and into "I can." You do that through reframing limiting Stories. I'm not talking about reciting positive affirmations and hoping for the best! I'm talking about really noticing those moments when a fear-based Story comes up and consciously deciding to reframe it as something that counteracts that fear and story. For example, if the fear-based Story is *It'll take too long to make that dream come true,* you could reframe it as *Even if it takes a while to make this dream happen, I'll go after it because my happiness is worth it.* When you learn how to reframe limiting Stories, you'll learn how to build a bridge between the parts of yourself that feel like what you want is far out of reach, the parts of yourself that are truly limitless, and the parts of yourself that know that with enough hard work and courage, change is possible.

Create community. What's the number one factor that can reinforce a habit? Being among people who also practice the same
habits. Some people reading this book already have a support
system that they can lean on, which is full of people who would
be excited to help them work to build their courage, while others
have loved ones but not necessarily people who would be interested in or supportive of their efforts to change. You'll learn how
to handle the opinions of others in ways that don't derail your
own progress, as well as how to find and make more connections
with like-minded people who also want to live more courageous,
authentic, and happier lives.

We'll complete this process with a reflection on what has
shifted. After all that work, it's always inspiring to look back and
see how far you've come and realize just how many limits and
doubts you busted through. It's truly exciting to see that the life
that you've been longing for can come to fruition much faster
than you might have realized just by using these tools. Meaningful
life change doesn't need to take forever! Change begins the
moment you apply the Courage Habit tools to your life.

I suggest that you keep a special notebook for taking notes as
you read through *The Courage Habit* and complete its exercises.
There's also a website for the book at http://www.yourcourageous
life.com/courage-habit where you can download worksheets that
accompany this book, as well as bonus audio.

From Fear to Courage

Typical self-help advice for "becoming more courageous" asks
people to attempt to ignore their fears or doubts by reciting affirmations to "stay positive" or by ordering the Critic inside to shut
up and go away. You won't find those suggestions in this book,

because, quite simply, none of them work long-term. If they did, no one would ever be afraid, because we've all tried those methods for handling our doubts and fears. Instead of exhausting yourself with fighting fear, this book starts with how you can be authentic, in charge of your own life, and trust yourself. You decide what your courageous life looks like and what your most courageous self wants to be, do, and experience. Then, you use the Courage Habit steps to create exactly that life. You get to see it come to fruition!

At the outset, most people I talk to about this process feel a little curious, maybe even hopeful, but still a bit dubious. I'll never forget working with Alexis, who connected with me as part of a corporate training program. In our sessions, I noticed that when Alexis talked about work, it was clear she truly loved it. However, she constantly second-guessed herself when it came to pitching new ideas that could have others seeing her as an innovator in her role as a project manager. She wanted the company to change how it was communicating with lower-level employees. She was wanting a more heart-based approach in the office culture that would leave room for everyone to voice their opinions. But, as she said to me, "Who the hell am I to tell the heads of the company that the entire system for how things are done should be changed? And if I told anyone in corporate America to be more 'heart-centered,' they'd laugh me out of the boardroom."

Like so many of us, Alexis had spent years thinking, "If I didn't feel so afraid, I'd tell them what I really think/make that change/take that big step." She had always assumed that for her to do the things she longed to do, she'd first need to figure out how to make her fear go away. Alexis was smart, and she'd tried plenty of "strategies" for getting her fear to go away, but she hadn't tried to really understand her fear deeply. That's where we began our work.

Starting with the Courage Habit step of accessing the body, Alexis got to know her fear and learned to identify exactly what was happening in those moments when she almost spoke up, yet stopped herself. Instead of trying to run from what her fear was telling her, she began to face it by listening to what the fearful voices were saying. This practice of "listening without attachment" revealed to Alexis that while the critical voices were condescending and often loud, that didn't mean that she had to do what they said. From there, she "reframed" the limiting, fear-based Stories that she'd told herself about what the higher-ups would think of her ideas: "Even if my ideas are judged, they are worth sharing. I can't know for sure how anyone will react." Then Alexis began to create community by floating her ideas to the coworkers she knew best, and then all of them collectively sat down for a meeting with the department head to lay out their thoughts on shifting communication with lower-level employees. Their courage in speaking up as a group bolstered Alexis's confidence. "Guess what," she said, when we met for a session a few months later. "They listened to us!"

Through using the four parts of the Courage Habit, Alexis changed the old cycle of running from her fears or self-doubt. Using her new understanding of habit-formation, she was no longer hoping for a moment of inspiration to hit when it would feel easy to speak up. Instead, she could use each step of the Courage Habit to see where fear or doubt was stopping her, see this as an old habituated routine, and decide to do something differently.

Chances are that right now you have something you'd very much like to change in your own life. Maybe, like Alexis, aspects of your job might not feel fulfilling. Or, perhaps you know that you give too much weight to what family members think, and you want to be braver about speaking up for yourself. Maybe you've got a personal dream that you've longed to fulfill, like traveling the entire world on a one-way ticket. Or maybe you want to do more to change the problems that the world faces. Possibly you're like I was when I realized that I didn't want to stay in my old career, and that tipped off a scary but necessary process of looking at who I *really* was and what I wanted my life to be about.

The clients I've worked with all have different goals or want different things, but what they have in common is that they are tired of fear or self-doubt running their lives. They're tired of waiting for the day when they'll somehow "feel courageous enough" to make a change, and they want to start taking effective actions for following their dreams.

When you start to practice each of the four Courage Habit parts, your most courageous self begins calling the shots, not your fear. You don't have to wait to start living with more courage. It's something you can begin, today.

The Question Before You

I know how hard this work can be. I have personally made mistakes and had trouble trusting this process. However, I also know that going after what you most desire, facing fear along the way, and seeing your courageous life come to fruition is absolutely possible. As you're integrating what you learn, take care not to get caught in what I call the "self-help hamster wheel," where you're running and spinning furiously as you try to "improve." Like most of my clients, I spent years "working on myself," reading self-help books, and attending workshops, hoping that they would "fix" me. Fear was the identified problem, and I spent a long time hoping that if I could chant away, meditate away, logically reason away, or fight away my fears, I'd finally feel I was good enough. I now see that model as an old model, one that is particularly sold to women. That model prioritizes logic over emotion and intuition, and striving to achieve perfection to be considered "successful."

Instead, the Courage Habit model is about learning to be with the things that are uncomfortable and living from a place of wholeness. It's about embracing the fear *and* the courage, the doubt *and* the success, the expansion *and* the contraction, and fundamentally trusting in your own resilience, capacity, and goodness along the way. These are the heart-based conversations that I'm having with coaching clients, where we talk about life not as a series of goals to meet, but as a process to engage with.

Learning to engage with a process takes time, presence, adjustment, and refinement. I still regularly encounter fear as I go after the things I want in life, speak up about injustice, or face critics. I believe that if I didn't continue to regularly practice the tools that are available to me through the Courage Habit, I would come to feel stuck all over again. As you're going through this process, you'll need some way to practice pieces of the Courage Habit process daily. When I was first struggling with change and wanted to keep myself accountable, I created a small grid in the back of a notebook and tracked with a simple checkmark if I had taken a few minutes for the things I needed to do, like accessing my body to see what I was really feeling or reframing limiting Stories when they cropped up. Someone else might decide that gold stars on a sheet of paper or digital apps with reminder prompts are more their speed for making sure they are accountable about doing the daily work. It doesn't matter what you choose; it just matters that you choose something that will honestly reinforce this work in your daily life.

The most courageous work you'll ever do is being willing to look squarely at who you are, the life you are creating, and to change course if you aren't happy. Is the life you're living right now a life that you'll look back on and be proud of? Are words like *joy* the first that you'll use to describe how your life feels? I want these to be your new metrics for a happy, fulfilled life. You only get this one life. It matters that you live it well. You matter. Your dreams matter.

The question before you is: Will you choose to identify and shift any fear-based ways of living in favor of creating your courageous life? We can keep people-pleasing, pushing ourselves, trying to avoid self-doubt, hesitating in the face of change, shying away from taking that chance on a long-held dream, or we can decide that we deserve more.

We can learn to let go of what others think, and give ourselves permission to live how we want to live. We can decide that we're sick of the status quo and step off the tracks we've been on, and develop the courage to trust in our capacity to figure out a better way to live. We can learn how to have the courage to speak up, creating change in our relationships, in our communities, and in our world. We can prioritize being real and honest, and find other people in the world who hold those as their highest values as well. This requires looking honestly at your fears, and then deciding how you'll practice courage. You're capable of doing it. The question is this: What will you choose?

Chapter 1

Your Most Courageous Self

It's safe to say that we've all been there—that place where you know that something in your job, relationship, or life in general is definitely not working, but you don't know what the alternative would be. When I realized that the lifestyle I'd hustled so hard for wasn't a reflection of who I really was, it also dawned on me that I didn't know what to replace it with. I didn't really know who I was or know what I truly wanted. More than anything, I felt afraid to make a step in *any* direction, because I wasn't sure I could trust myself to make sound decisions. After all, wasn't I the one who'd made all the choices that had landed me in this position? When I was making decision after decision about my life up to that point, I'd been convinced that I was moving in the direction of what I wanted, only to discover that it was anything but.

When I dug a little deeper into examining the choices I'd made, I realized that for years, I *hadn't* been convinced that I was moving in the direction of what I wanted. In hindsight, I could see multiple points where I had been ignoring signals from my body and my intuition, routinely choosing options based on what people thought of me or how great I hoped I would look, rather than listening to my own internal compass.

Shifting from external cues to internal cues is tough work, which is why so many of us avoid doing it if we can. My highly logical and pragmatic self was now trying to tune in to vague, hard-to-articulate desires for change, and I often felt conflicted. A part of me still wanted order and routine and a neat little path to follow, even if it hadn't led to happiness thus far. At least that was a path that I, and everyone around me, understood. I didn't want to be one of those people who "listened to her body's wisdom." And, intuition? *Puh-lease.* I wasn't going to try to listen to something that science couldn't even prove existed!

The problem was that I was trying to cling to some sense of safety and control by immediately mapping out a new plan to replace my old one. I wanted to both "dream big" and "be realistic" at the same time, which wasn't getting me anywhere. It was time to go beyond clinging to some sense of control by mapping things out in advance. Whatever plan came next for my life, it had to first be founded in who I really was and what I truly wanted, and that meant asking the harder questions of deep self-inquiry.

We've all felt the push and pull of this space. We want radical change, but we also want practical plans. We can have both of those things, just not at the same time, and that's why beginning with discovering who you truly are and what you truly want is so important for any process of change. We need to ask the questions that require us to take an honest look at ourselves and our lives: *Who am I, really? What do I really want? What does a happy life look like for me? How will I make who I truly am on the inside be how I live on the outside?*

Getting honest about questions like these is how I begin every coaching relationship. In asking the right questions, possibilities start to open up and an aspect of the self that might have long been dormant starts to emerge. It's what I call your "most courageous self."

This chapter seeks to explore those sorts of questions, starting with this big one: *What do you deeply, truly want for your life?* However you answer that question opens the door to exploring your most courageous self—her way of being, what she values, what arouses her delight, and the experiences that she most wants to have. This most courageous self is already within all of us. We aren't working hard to turn ourselves "into" our most courageous selves, so much as we need to clear away the stuff (like being paralyzed by self-doubt) that has covered over that self, preventing her from being able to show up.

The exercises in this chapter will range from telling the truth about what is not working, to exploring your wildest dreams, to getting real about your own personal integrity. In many ways, what you uncover will be like receiving a big permission slip that you write for yourself to stop buying into obligation and "shoulds," and start defining what a free, joyful, and courageous life looks like. When your most courageous self emerges, who you truly are on the inside gets to step forward and become how you live on the outside.

Who Is Your Most Courageous Self?

In coaching, we try to get as specific as possible about what a person desires so that we can start creating a map for how to get there. Clients, workshop participants, and seminar attendees have described wanting to live their lives in the following ways:

- Be able to clarify how they want to feel and make decisions that will cultivate more of those feelings.

- Follow their curiosity and delight, even if it means stepping outside of their comfort zones or encountering criticism.

- Be open to new experiences even if there are no guaranteed outcomes.

- Develop more resilience through a willingness to make mistakes.

- Consistently ask themselves what courageous action would look like and acting in accordance with that.

- Remain committed to believing that they can do the things that they want to do despite the challenges, and actively pursuing the resources they need to do that.

- Use their growth to help others or give back in some way.

These desires are completely in alignment with *courage psychology*, an emerging discipline that seeks to understand how people cultivate and practice courage in their lives. In 2007, researchers even developed a theoretical model of what a person's courageous mindset looks like, and it includes all these states and traits collectively pulled together (Hannah, Sweeney, and Lester 2010). With that said, your most courageous self isn't just a compilation of traits; she's how those traits are *expressed*, and that's what makes all the difference.

Take, for instance, Shay, a yoga instructor who tapped into her most courageous self at one of my workshops. Months later, she reached out to share that it had completely revolutionized her approach to teaching yoga. Before clarifying who her most courageous self was, she had been like many other yoga teachers, offering a gentle, breathy "Namaste" at the end of class and reminding people to "Be at one with the pose." After the workshop with me, Shay said, "My most courageous self is—excuse my French—a fucking badass. I realized that the type of yoga I wanted to offer to people was the kind where I called them out a bit. I'd start saying in classes, 'People, stop avoiding the poses you don't like. Get in there, and do the pose to the best of your ability, but don't cop out on yourself.' I still remember the first time that I ever said that in a class, and how it felt like this rush. It was so different than anything else I'd ever seen in the yoga world. I literally went out and bought a leather moto jacket after things changed. And, people dig it, and my classes are *always* full. My most courageous self pushes me, and so I push the students to not be complacent and not to skip out on the stuff we're resistant to just because that's easier."

Shay also realized that one of the areas where she'd been complacent had been in her love life. She had been living with her boyfriend Malcolm for several years, and while she wanted to get married, he resisted commitment. For Shay's new, increasingly bolder self, it no longer worked for her to be complacent in that relationship. She and Malcolm ended up making the painful decision to break up. "Now I'm dating, again," Shay shared with me. "And sometimes it sucks. But, it's like I tell my students: don't skip out on the hard stuff, on the poses you don't like. Now I'm doing things that I would never have even considered when I was in a relationship, like I got invited to coteach a yoga teacher training for an entire month in Bali this spring. And, I can do it. I can pack up and go whenever I want. I feel like I'm being myself."

Being your most courageous self doesn't always have to be as bold as Shay's approach. My client Ellen, a sales rep who regularly traveled and gave presentations to clients for her job, expressed that her deepest desire was just to have time to herself and read every book she'd ever put off reading. Initially, I suspected Ellen's desire to spend more time reading was just her need to rest and recuperate after years of *going-going-going*, and that other, bolder dreams would emerge once she'd given herself that time. But, as it turned out, that *was* Ellen's dream. Ellen ended up creating a life where she could have exactly what she wanted—plenty of time to read. She quit her job and moved into a "tiny house," a small mobile trailer encompassing only 250 square feet, reducing her costs significantly. Even though this simplified life could be measured by conventional standards as a meager one, this was Ellen's ultimate expression of her most courageous self.

"Every time I asked myself what a good life looked like, it always included reading more books and talking about books with other people," Ellen said. "That's what really got me excited. For so long, I didn't let myself have that because it wasn't giving something back or contributing somehow. But, when I really tuned in to what I wanted the most, I realized that I didn't even know who that person was... I'm not very social. I'm quiet. It's how I always was as a kid. My nose was always stuck in a book. I wanted it to be stuck in a book again." Later, Ellen went back to school to get her master's in literature to be able to talk shop about books in an environment with others who loved the written word.

Shay and Ellen were both cultivating the same courageous qualities, just in different ways. Each woman was clarifying what she truly wanted and following what delighted her. They were both willing to follow unknown paths, make mistakes, and ask themselves along the way what courageous action would look like. They were encountering challenges with a willingness to believe that they'd find their way through. However, how the qualities that comprise courageous living were *expressed* for each woman was markedly different since both women were defining their lives by what was uniquely important to them. Shay's path involved getting more "badass" and more vocal about what she truly believed, while Ellen's path had been one of getting quieter and creating more space for going within. At the outset of making these shifts, both women were just as afraid of taking the risks that naturally come with change. But, both women decided that they were no longer willing to settle for anything less than living in alignment with who they truly knew they were.

Imagining a Liberated Day

One of my favorite exercises to assign clients also opened up the most insight for me when I was trying to figure out how to shift my own life. It is called the "Liberated Day" exercise. You sit down and map out a bold, full-tilt day where you're living in exactly the way that you wish you were living, with nothing held back and incredible detail about every nuance. One of the best things about this exercise is that it will help you to sink into courageous living as a way of being, rather than as a series of things "to do."

As you do the exercise, be careful of "dreaming big" while also trying to "be realistic." This is a place where I got stuck when I first did this exercise. This exercise is the opportunity to give yourself the ultimate permission slip to write down a vision of your life exactly as you want it, with no holds barred and no need to reign yourself in by "being realistic." If your fear tells you that you're "asking for too much," or that what you're writing about goes beyond the limits of money or time that you have available, this is a rare moment when I'll tell you to ignore your fear and write down even the things that seem like you're "asking for too much." If you reign yourself in or tell yourself to be "realistic" about time or money during this process, you're only ever going to create a reigned-in, realistic kind of a life. Go bigger. You'll sort out details of how to create this kind of a life later. For now, stay with the big vision.

You can use a sheet of paper to answer these questions, or head to http://www.yourcourageouslife.com/courage-habit to access the "Liberated Day" worksheet.

Liberated Day

Think about this question: *If you woke up tomorrow and your entire life went exactly the way that you wanted it to go, from morning until night, what would that day look like?* Describe it from start to finish.

Describe *how* you wake up. *Where* do you wake up? How do you *feel* when you wake up? What are you looking forward to when you wake up?

Tell us about any other rituals that would guide your morning.

Tell us about the work you'd be doing. Let's assume for this exercise that there's some kind of work that doesn't even feel like "work," because it's pleasurable. It's work that lights you up.

Who are you interacting with during the day? What kind of people? What are they interested in that meshes with what you're interested in?

Tell us about your afternoon, then your evening.

What are some things that you'd be giving back to the world as part of living this life? How would this day have a greater purpose?

What are the passion projects that you make time for during the day? What are the "fun things" that you do "just because," rather than from a goal-directed place?

Tell us about who you live with.

Tell us about how you express your creative longings.

Tell us about how you relax and wind down.

Describe how you feel as you sink into bed at the end of the day—a day in which you've lived a life in alignment with your most courageous self.

People describe all sorts of reactions to the "Liberated Day" exercise. Some leave it feeling excited, and they eagerly begin writing down all sorts of grand plans. Some people immediately start questioning themselves: Did they write down the "right" thing? Did they do the exercise "correctly"? Others worry that what they've articulated isn't bold enough.

Here's what I share about the exercise: It is just a doorway to thinking about courageous living as a way of being. In other words, it's less about making specific plans to conform your life to what you've written down, and more about an opportunity to think outside the box while honoring the value of courage. People who live courageous lives aren't necessarily people who sell everything and move to a new country or start skydiving and getting into adventure sports.

While those examples require courage as action and involve facing fears, the truly courageous life is one where a person's "way of being" in the world reflects the value of courage. In thinking about courage as a way of being, you're being asked to honor the value of courage and treat "courage" as one of your most highly prioritized personal values.

Honoring the Value of Courage

Honoring courage as a value means that the choices you make take those courageous qualities into account and put them into action—no skydiving required! If you're a stay-at-home mom who has no intention of selling everything she owns to move to another country, honoring courage as a value could mean asking how you want to feel on a hard parenting day and making choices that align with that. If your dream is to crack the C-suite at your company, you might honor the value of courage by being willing to take risks that involve making mistakes, trusting that you will find your way through.

When you're honoring the value of courage, you're regularly and routinely asking yourself, "If my most courageous self was making the decision here, what would I choose?" That's the question that Ellen was asking herself when she decided to downsize her life, and go back to school for no reason other than because she wanted to. That's the question that Shay was asking herself, when she rocked a moto jacket, changed how she ran her yoga classes, and decided to end a stagnant relationship rather than stay just because it was comfortable. These two women each honored the value of courage in their actions, and courage as a "way of being" was underlying their processes.

Sometimes, people feel more uncertain than they do excited after completing this exercise. Others share that they don't feel uncertainty, so much as they just don't feel much of anything and it was hard to get into the process. If you're one of those people, this is okay, too. Fear shows up in many ways, and feelings of uncertainty, discomfort, or reluctance to get into the process are just manifestations of fear. This means that something deep within you recognizes that change is at hand and something is at stake in your life. The fact that you're able to notice this discomfort will be a very valuable part of shifting fears or self-doubt that hold you back. As you continue through each chapter of this book, you'll meet several people who struggled with various aspects of the process, but they transformed their lives because they stopped thinking of fear or discomfort as some kind of sign to stop moving forward. Every single one of them completed this exercise and wondered if this was the time that things were really going to be different. Instead of letting those doubts stop them, they decided to keep moving in the direction of changing their lives. They got to the other side and found out exactly how capable they really were.

Others may have finished this exercise feeling excited about what's possible, accompanied by a sense of indecision or of being overwhelmed about what comes next. It's normal to go back and forth about what you want. You've been doing things the old way for a long time and now you're contemplating new possibilities, which would arouse doubt or uncertainty for anyone. The bottom line? Doubt, uncertainty, and wondering if you're "doing it right" is par for the course. As you'll see in later chapters, simply being willing to notice what comes up for you is going to be the start of rerouting some very old patterns. If you're attuning to what you feel in your body during this process, you're already doing some of the work!

Before we can go more in-depth with the Courage Habit work, it's important that we take a moment to actively apply this principle of "honoring the value of courage" to your life. To make the process easier and more focused, I'm going to ask you to start applying the personal value of courage to different areas, using the question, "What would be different in this area of my life if my most courageous self was running the show?" Then, after looking at each area, see what you notice about the whole. It can be helpful to write your answers for these exercises down, though you can just think about them too. (If you'd like to download a worksheet version of this exercise, you can find it at http://www .yourcourageouslife.com/courage-habit.)

Honoring the Value of Courage

Fun and Recreation: What would be different about your spare time if your most courageous self was running the show? In other words, what would you do with your spare time if you could base it solely on your interests and didn't worry about whether what you chose to do looked cool or was the "most efficient" way to spend your time?

Career and Work: If your most courageous self was calling the shots with the work you do to sustain your life and lifestyle, what would that look like? It can be especially useful to think of any areas of work that you desire to transition into, or the career you dream of having.

Money: How would your most courageous self be spending money? We're going to consider money separately from career and work for the purposes of this exercise, so that you can examine exactly how you save and spend it, and whether that's what your courageous self would do.

Family Relationships: What would be different in your relationships with members of your immediate family, such as parents or your siblings? If you have children, how does this courageous self approach parenting? Romantic relationships and friendships are considered separately.

Romantic Relationships and Sensuality: This category encompasses a partner or marriage if you are in a committed relationship, as well as your overall feelings about your sensuality, and can include dating if you are not in a committed relationship. How are things different in your romantic life if your most courageous self is at the helm?

Friendships: This category includes all manner of friends, from the people you've known the longest to coworkers that you wish you knew better. Consider how you'd be connecting with these friendships from the vantage point of your most courageous self.

Health and Body: This category is all about the physical body and can include everything from how rested, exercised, and nourished your body is to how you're treating ongoing illnesses.

Physical Environment: This category is all about your actual physical living space itself and what your most courageous self would do to create a space that feels more like "you," including addressing any conflicts with others who live in that space with you.

Personal Growth and Development: This category includes personal goals or ways that you've wanted to push yourself. For instance, maybe you've always wanted to write a book or run a marathon. It can also include feelings that you wish you felt more often. For example, you might say, "If my most courageous self were running the show, I know that I'd feel more grounded and less overwhelmed" or "I'd feel confident about making decisions."

For the last step of this exercise, please review what you've written and notice if anything jumps out at you. You're looking for those items that have a bit of sizzle, the ones that make you think: "Ooooh, it would scare me to do that, but if it all worked out for the best, that would be an amazing life!" Highlight anything that has that kind of draw for you, taking it as a sign that a bolder part of yourself would love to emerge in that area.

Establishing the Primary Focus

Now that you've finished the "Liberated Day" and "Honoring the Value of Courage" exercises, you've considered many different possibilities for what your more courageous life can look like. Some of them will be small scale. Some of them will be pretty radical!

Since the idea of a complete life overhaul is impractical—not to mention terrifying—I often encourage people to identify just three things that they'd like to shift, treating them as a Primary Focus for practicing the steps of the Courage Habit throughout the rest of this book. I suggest narrowing it to three things so that you can work on small, digestible pieces of making life changes, instead of trying to do too much at once.

The Primary Focus can consist of both tangible goals that have clear outcomes (that is, cook every recipe in an Alice Waters cookbook, spend two weeks in Morocco, and so forth) and more intangible goals (that is, reconnect to who I know I truly am, understand the patterns that broke up my marriage, and so on). People usually choose a mixture of both, understanding that even though we're using language that refers to goals or being action oriented, we're really talking about how you want to feel about yourself and your life as you're taking action. If you're writing down the three things for your Primary Focus and feel enlivened, turned on, a little nervous, and completely excited, you're going in the right direction.

If you already know exactly what your three Primary Focus items would be, great! Go ahead and write them down. If it all feels big and you want a bit of help honing in on your three items, there are a few different approaches that you could take to clarifying your own Primary Focus. Read through each of these to see which approach appeals to you the most, and then pick one to try. To avoid feeling overwhelmed, choose just one and complete it. "Done" is better than "perfect."

Curiosity, excitement, and delight. Review your responses to either the "Most Courageous Self" or "Liberated Day" and note what brings up any feelings of excitement, curiosity, and delight, even if it's just the faintest glimmer. Underline or highlight those items, and choose three. When Shay was reviewing what she wrote for her "Liberated Day," she noticed that she had jotted down something about getting up in the morning and throwing on a black leather moto jacket. The image of that jacket aroused her curiosity and delight when she was further narrowing her Primary Focus. Following this small glimmer of a detail was part of thinking outside the box about her way of being as a yoga teacher.

Where do you want to be? Review what you wrote from either of the exercises, keeping in mind the question "What would I want my life to be like six months from now?" Underline or highlight anything that has you think, "If my life was like this six months from now, that would be amazing!" Again, aim for three things.

Consult your most courageous self. In the same way that you honored the value of courage in different life categories, you could apply this globally to your life by asking, "What three things would I be doing differently if my most courageous self was running the show?"

The stop-doing list. Sometimes, we need to "back into" what we want by first articulating what we don't want to do any longer. What are you fed up with? What's slowly draining your energy? Make the list of things that you want to stop doing. Then, review what you wrote for the past two exercises, particularly looking for the opposite things that you might start doing. For instance, if "being in debt" is on your stop-doing list as something you're fed up with, you'd review the last two exercises for ways of living with courage that would take you out of debt. This is exactly how Ellen started thinking outside the box when she decided to move into a tiny house.

Remember, to make the above changes easeful and sustainable, it's important that you narrow them down. Choose three things that you'd like to keep as a Primary Focus for the duration of your work with the Courage Habit. If you feel like you really need just one more, remember that when you've completed the Courage Habit process, you can always go back for another round. You'll be more successful at seeing change if you put all your effort into just a few things that excite you, rather than spreading yourself thin.

Your Reason Why

It's not uncommon for someone to have at least a moment's hesitation at this juncture. On one hand, you might feel excited about finally creating the life that you've dreamed of having. On the other hand, you might be worrying that you're wanting "too much."

"I feel selfish," one client, Janelle, told me. Her Primary Focus was releasing herself from the pressure to be an on-call, endlessly devoted, twenty-four-seven mom, and start to reclaim who she was before she became a mother. What Janelle shared echoed what I've heard from other women, all of whom received the same messages from society—that it's selfish for women, and particularly for mothers, to focus on or meet one's own needs.

Here's the thing: The desire to live with more courage in one's own life doesn't have to come down to a choice between benefiting the self versus benefiting others. In my review of the research about how people change, I ran across something that fascinated me. In a 2009 study on self-identity, researchers found that the goal-setting process could be more successful when goals benefited not just the individual, but also the collective. The researchers labeled goals that benefited only the individual as "self-image goals," and goals that benefited both the individual as well as others as "compassionate goals." Researchers found that compassionate goals were more attainable, in part because the goal setter was more motivated to stay the course knowing that others would benefit. Compassionate goals also resulted in goal setters who were happier with the results they'd achieved, once they'd arrived at their goal (Crocker, Olivier, and Neur 2009).

It's pretty cool to think that if you connect the changes you're making to how they will benefit you and the wider world, you'll not only do good for others, you're also more likely to be successful at changing and you'll feel happier once you've made those changes. I think the same can be true of the "goal" of shifting your life to live with more courage, leaving old fear patterns behind. As you become more courageous, your life improves, as do the lives of those around you.

Take some time, now, to think about how your Primary Focus benefits not just you but also the people around you and the wider world. For instance, if your Primary Focus is to travel the world, who are all the people who benefit? Initially, you might think you are the only person who benefits. But if you expand your view a bit, you can see more. For instance, on a purely pragmatic level, how will your travels contribute to the local economies of the places you travel to? On a more visionary level, maybe you've been feeling like life is devoid of joy, and traveling the world is the adventure of a lifetime that lifts you out of that. You can't draw water from a well that's dry, and if that travel adventure fills your internal reserves again, that reconnection to your personal happiness will positively impact the lives of those around you. Perhaps, because you're happier, you'll have more capacity for supporting family members when they're struggling, you'll be a better team player at work, or you'll feel like you finally have the energy to start doing more volunteer work. Remember what I shared in the introduction: unhappiness and discontent are signals that something is off in life, and they are worth paying attention to.

Are there benefits for your partner, children, job, or anyone else because you decide to bring forth your most courageous self? Will feeling braver in your personal life make you feel braver about speaking out on the issues that matter to you? Will giving to yourself make you feel like you have more to offer others? When I talk to people about this and hear their stories of how they reclaimed something essential to who they were and then found it within themselves to start giving back more to others, the answer to these questions is yes.

Women in particular are tasked with endless self-sacrifice and giving. So, let me clarify that this isn't about making your goals more palatable for others by tying them to service. Rather, I'm pointing out that as you decide how you want to shift your life, the research indicates that when you can make a connection between doing good for you and doing good for others, *everyone* is happier, and everyone wins.

Expanding your "reason why I'm changing my life" to include the benefits to others can also become a powerful motivator when challenges arise. You'll be more motivated to keep going even when fear or self-doubt are raging, because your desire to change isn't just about you.

There's something very big at stake if you decide to give up on living a life that really means something to you—the world would never be able to experience the gifts that you have to offer.

A life lived with courage is, hands down, a more joyful life. You're stepping into the adventure of being fully alive in the ups and downs, fun, and challenges. The process of shifting into your most courageous self will of course bring difficult things, but more importantly, it'll bring *oh-my-god-amazing* things. We've all heard the saying, "Everything you want is on the other side of your fear." In the pages that come, you're going to directly experience how that is true.

Chapter 2

Habits and Courage

I once led a workshop on tapping into your deepest desires where a woman said, "I just wish I didn't feel so afraid." From across the room, another woman piped up, "You and me both, sister!" After that, the woman who had spoken up first went from having a face drawn with tension to one of laughter, and then the entire room was laughing together. It was the most ridiculous thing, wasn't it? We all just wanted to not feel afraid when pursuing our dreams. Why can't it be that simple?

It can't be that simple because bypassing any one emotion is just not how humans are hardwired. As shame researcher and author Dr. Brené Brown puts it, "You can't selectively shut down emotion." Emotions are a package deal, which means that if you try to shut down just your fear, you're also clamping down on your capacity to feel joy.

While it would certainly be easier if we could just do away with emotions that are more uncomfortable, fear (or self-doubt, stress, hesitation—fear goes by many names) is a normal part of taking a risk. There isn't a single openhearted, curious, and emotionally available person who isn't also able to acknowledge at least *something* that has a fearful, uncertain edge for them.

Fearlessness is a myth. Admitting to having fears doesn't mean that someone's fundamentally insecure. Rather, admitting to experiencing fear or self-doubt is a healthy part of the process of change and going after the things that matter the most.

Trying to become fearless is a wasted effort on the path to making your deepest desires come to fruition. Paradoxically, it's fully understanding and *claiming* your fear that stops it from having power over any part of your life. That's exactly what we'll be exploring in this chapter. You'll get a clear picture of how fear and self-doubt operate by learning some of the science behind habit-formation. You'll see why fear can feel so intense and why the impulse to back down usually feels so automatic, almost as if it can't be helped. You'll learn that, in fact, it can be helped. I'll be offering you the same supportive guidance I offer the clients that I coach. In addition, I'll be sharing the stories of others who have done this work so that you can see that you're not alone.

Armed with information about the brain, as well as the cues, routines, and rewards that can fuel either patterns of fear or courage, you'll be able to see exactly how you've become stuck in the past and will be able to chart a new path by making immediate choices about how you want to live your life. When the Courage Habit is practiced regularly, you'll stop getting stuck in the old patterns of fear or self-doubt, and start seeing real change happen.

The Power of Habit

In Chapter 1, you defined your Primary Focus by identifying three things that you want to shift while you complete this book. If you haven't already felt some doubt or hesitation arise, you'll most likely experience those feelings once you start taking action toward your focus. If you already know that you'll inevitably encounter fear and that you can't bypass it, the question then becomes: How will you successfully work through it?

A desire for change and willpower alone isn't enough. There are processes in the brain governing habit-formation that play a key role in how we respond to feelings of fear—something that most of us have never considered. First, let me give you a little run-down in how current science tells us that habits form. Habit-formation is predominantly a three-part process. (Prepare to geek out, because this gets pretty cool.) There's a *cue*, which is like a trigger that sets things off. There's a *routine*, which is a set of behaviors or responses to that trigger. Routines are designed to get to the reward, which is the relief you feel when the tension dies down.

We typically think of "habits" in terms of "doing" something—the habit of exercising, flossing, or checking your email after you arrive at work. We work through cue-routine-reward loops all day long when we interact with family and friends, at home and on the job, in line at the grocery store, or sitting in front of a computer. Some cues are quite benign, such as hearing your alarm clock in the morning and feeling the cue to begin waking yourself up. Other cues, of course, are more difficult to experience. For example, a coworker's criticism or a partner's drinking problem can cue feelings of fear or self-doubt. When working with cue-routine-reward loops, the question is: How do we interrupt the loops that aren't helpful for our lives?

In *The Power of Habit* (2014), writer Charles Duhigg notes that it's not just the things we want to do that are governed by the cue-routine-reward process. Many of our *emotional* experiences in life follow that same cue-routine-reward pathway, including how we experience fear and then respond to that fear.

That's precisely what Yasmine noticed when she began taking action. As we worked together to define her Primary Focus, one item felt particularly bold: "Find a studio space." After years of painting in a small corner of her kitchen, she wanted to rent professional studio space and start creating large-scale pieces, maybe even murals. At first, she felt nothing but excited, but the moment she stepped through the door of a large warehouse with artists' spaces for a tour with the manager, she felt panic.

Standing there, faced with the cubicle dividers separating each artist's station, she found herself suddenly feeling stupid. "I kept thinking, *you're not a real artist; it would be so stupid to waste money renting space*," she told me. "I got the hell out of there as quickly as I could. The manager probably thought I was crazy. Talking about this now, I know that I should have just given it a chance. But, in the moment, it felt like too much."

The sensation of fear and discomfort was a cue in Yasmine's body. For many years, she had responded to that cue with a routine to avoid the uncomfortable thing to get to the quickest possible reward that would bring about a release of tension. That's the important connection to make with cue-routine-reward! In any given moment, when our self-doubt is loud and intense, we are hardwired to try to get to the fastest possible release of tension even when that option is counter to our larger life desires.

When I say "hardwired," I'm talking about the process of cue-routine-reward as it originates in a part of the brain called the basal ganglia. Think of the basal ganglia as being like "command central" for behavior. The basal ganglia picks up what's happening in your body and in your environment and determines what you should do to deal with it. When it feels fear or self-doubt, its mission becomes to release the tension those emotions cause. Based on what's been effective in the past, it suggests routines that will get you to that release of tension the fastest. Those routines can take any number of forms, but the logic that leads the basal ganglia to choose them is the same—to avoid whatever fear-causing or self-doubt-causing thing you encountered.

Here's an example of the cue-routine-reward process:

Cue: Feeling afraid

Routine: Shying away from taking action (such as Yasmine's reaction at the studio space)

Reward: Temporarily decreased stress, now that the pressure's off

Every time we follow the basal ganglia's impulses and act out those same routines, we reinforce the entire cycle. The brain learns that avoidance (or whatever the habitual fear-based routine is) is effective at relieving tension. The basal ganglia notes that and will turn to that impulse again.

Does that mean that we're at the mercy of the cue-routine-reward loop? Thankfully, no! Ultimately, the basal ganglia's automation of behavior through cue-routine-reward loops has a positive purpose: it keeps us from having to think so hard about every single little choice in order to save brain power throughout the day. Because you want to make life changes that involve taking bold actions, you need to understand how this loop functions and use it to reinforce courageous actions instead of fear-based routines.

Duhigg's review of research on habit-formation indicates something very important for anyone who wants to change this cycle: if our emotional lives are influenced by cue-routine-reward and we want to change something, the most effective point of change is to change the *routine*. If you think about it, this makes sense. We can't control all aspects of life to avoid the stressful circumstances that "cue" us. Bills will need to be paid, critical people will walk into our lives, and systemic oppression (the opportunities we're denied because of gender, race, social class, or sexuality) is real. (This is why self-help programs that encourage you to pretend that challenges don't exist or to ignore your fear don't work—you'll always be laboring to ignore the fear!) It would be contrary to human nature to expect that anyone will stop wanting that "reward" of relief from feelings of fear or stress, so it would never work to try to change behavior without a corresponding reward. The most effective point of change is to think differently about how you *respond* to the cues you encounter.

Now, let's get to it! Let's look more closely at the cue-routine-reward loop, starting with the cue (the sensation of fear in the body) that triggers all the rest.

How Does Your Fear Show Up?

When I first met Eliana, she got straight to brass tacks: "I just need coaching for some help with time management and accountability," she told me briskly. I was working with her over the phone and had no clue what she looked like, but something about Eliana's tone suggested a woman in a power suit, perhaps Olivia Pope in the television show *Scandal*.

Eliana explained that she was finishing her MBA and working full-time for a consulting firm that required her to travel one week every month. I asked her to share more about why she decided to start coaching. She explained, "I've taken time-management classes, alphabetized and color-coded all of my files, and set up a million reminders on my phone, but it's not working. Basically, the reminders ding at me all day and as soon as I'm behind on just a few things, I stop even bothering to look at my phone. I don't have a fear problem. I have a time-management problem. Can you help with that?"

"Maybe," I said, adding, "As long as we're remaining open to the possibility that fear problems and time-management problems might have something in common."

Eliana laughed, "Sure, sure—I'm interested in whatever works. Just no psychoanalysis."

"Not with me," I said, smiling. "I've never been into Freud."

Together we began trying to understand what was happening for Eliana around time management. As the weeks went by and Eliana grew more comfortable sharing with me, our discussions about her attempts to get organized revealed something just a bit deeper. While she had a lot of outward accomplishments that everyone was impressed with, she constantly took on too much so that her colleagues would see her as a "team player." This made her feel overwhelmed, and was something she went to great lengths to hide. The feeling of being overwhelmed was exacerbated by her constantly checking and rechecking her work to make sure that she hadn't dropped any balls that could be noticed by others.

When I asked her what would be wrong with other people seeing her make a mistake, she replied as though it was obvious: "Because it's not professional and because then people wouldn't think I could handle everything." The trouble, of course, is that no one can handle everything. And if they try to? They experience overwhelm just like Eliana. I suspected that we were both aware of this, but I knew that the solutions weren't going to be as simple as telling her to "just stop" taking on more than she could handle. I thought I'd see if we could go a little bit deeper.

"What would happen if your coworkers saw that you couldn't handle everything?" I asked. There was a long silence on the phone.

"It would be embarrassing," she finally said. "Of course, there are the practical consequences. I might get passed over for the good projects or promotions. And, I'm the woman on my team— the only woman. All the guys band together. So, really, it would be embarrassing to make that kind of mistake and feel like no one has my back."

That was the first hint that there were dots to connect between what had appeared to be just a "time management problem" and fear. Eliana's fear was legitimately based in her observations of how women are treated in the corporate business world. For too long, she had been taking on more than she could handle and hiding her stress and feelings of being overwhelmed because she didn't want to be seen as "one of those emotional women" by her male colleagues.

"So, would it be safe to say that we've found where there's some fear happening?" I asked.

"Okay, okay, you win," she said, though I heard some shifting lightness in her voice and possibly a little relief. "So, *maybe* there's some fear there!"

As I grew more acquainted with Eliana's process, I kept noticing something interesting when we talked about the logistics of how she was getting things done. Out of her fear of missing something, Eliana often inserted extra steps into a process. For example, before she completed a homework assignment for one of her MBA classes, she decided that she had to update her computer's operating system and the word-processing software that was installed. Then she noticed that the external hard drive used for backups was almost full, so she decided that before she'd start the homework, she'd run to the Apple store and buy a new backup hard drive. Once that had taken an entire Saturday afternoon, she realized that she had skipped lunch and now it was dinner-time. Then, after she ate dinner she felt too tired to concentrate on homework.

After we had talked about the ins and outs of Eliana's day, I told her, "I wonder if fear is showing up differently than you would expect it to. You've shared that you don't really experience fear, and that you think of fear as being like…a *sensation* that's so over-powering that you wouldn't take action if you felt it. But in your case, could it be that when you feel fear it shows up as a felt sense of *urgency*? I think I'm hearing that when you feel a sensation of urgency in your body, you respond in ways that end up throwing you off course. The urgency is an intense feeling, a sensation in the body that carries some anxiety. It becomes easier to respond to that feeling with some small task, like updating your comput-er's software, rather than finishing the homework assignment. You're driven to get something, anything done, even if that means losing the larger priority."

When it was all laid out, Eliana confirmed that this is what was happening for her. This feeling of urgency that showed up anytime Eliana faced a task also brought anxiety, which made her feel these impulses to start proving herself. At the start, it always seemed like the logical option to respond to that feeling of urgency, to "just deal with it" so that it would go away. She didn't identify that sensation of urgency as "fear" because she thought of fear as being like that elevator-dropping sensation that people get when watching a scary movie, something that would keep her from taking action, whereas she was all about action. These feel-ings of urgency were her fears, and she was responding to them without questioning whether they were prompting her to do anything helpful, which led her down the rabbit hole of getting lost in smaller tasks and kept her from feeling accomplished or satisfied with the work she'd done.

Eliana thought that because she was a go-getter who went after what she wanted that all she had was a time-management problem, not a fear problem. It surprised her to realize how the urgency (the fear) was underlying other issues in her life. Examining those feelings of urgency became the starting ground for change for Eliana. In the months that followed, I worked with her to learn how to recognize the different ways that fear was showing up in her life. We enacted a specific series of steps in response that would change the cycle she'd felt stuck in for far too long.

Your experience of fear might be completely different than Eliana's, but like her, it may show up in ways that people wouldn't label as "fear." For instance, have you ever had trouble with chronic forgetting? That's a common way that we experience fear, only we think we're just "being forgetful." Feeling inexplicably irritated? For some people faced with pressure to keep it all together, instead of feeling urgency and an impulse to do something, the fear shows up as irritation with others, blaming them for why things feel so stressful. (Most of us have had bosses who responded to their own fear and stress by taking things out on employees in this way.) Some of my clients experience fear that arises physically as sudden exhaustion or with symptoms such as headaches or a health crisis. Other people have felt a kind of numbness come over themselves that they would describe as walking through their lives on autopilot or a "checking out" feeling that isn't clinical depression but that isn't right, either. No matter how your fear is expressed in your life, the one constant is that the fear keeps you from acting in ways that are aligned with living the life you truly want to live or taking the necessary steps to make your dreams come to fruition.

Consider this for yourself: What's your experience of fear like in the moment when you're in it? Remember, you can substitute other words for "fear" if that feels more resonant. You can call it "urgency," "self-doubt," or "nagging worries" if those labels feel more accurate. Just try to describe what it's like when you are in the real-time experience of fear. Do you tend to shut down, or, conversely, do you get hyperaware or push yourself harder? Do your thoughts come at you fast, or do you feel like you can't quite articulate anything in your head?

To get clear on how you uniquely experience fear, think about the last time you were in a fear-inducing situation. Maybe you were telling someone the truth about how you really felt, you were pitching an idea or asking for a favor, or you were on the receiving end of criticism from a boss or family member. When you were putting yourself on the line or when someone was upset with you, what was happening in your body? On paper, describe the fear sensations that you remember. What fear sensations do you experience? Where do they show up in your body? What happens once you become aware of them?

Like Eliana, recognizing how you uniquely experience sensations of fear will help you to recognize fear sensations as the cues that they are. What is the sensation like? What impulses come up again and again? Recognizing these fear sensation cues makes all the difference when we start changing our routines and shifting the entire cue-routine-reward loop. The sensations of fear that cue us can also be clues about what it is we are afraid of. That's what we'll explore in the next section

Clarifying Your Specific Fears

Now that you've taken time to observe and clarify the way sensations of fear show up in your body, we're going to get more specific. What are the specific fears, doubts, or worries that you're dealing with? Maybe it's being presented with situations where you don't know how to respond, where you might fail, feel vulnerable, lose a relationship, or perhaps face rejection. Or, maybe it's a fear that wanting more for your life will require giving up some of what you've currently got, and that could require too much sacrifice.

Clarifying Your Fears

Here are some questions to clarify some of your specific fears. Remember, everyone fears something. If your initial impulse is to think you don't fear anything, consider if that response is unconscious fear-avoidance, which is a way of diminishing feelings of fear by pretending that they don't exist or checking out from feeling them. If you remember, that was exactly how I handled my own fears for far too long and at great cost to my life and happiness. Even if you consider yourself to be an overachiever who seems to have no problem going after what she wants, dig a little deeper with the questions that follow. Odds are that no matter how much you've accomplished, there's still some place where fear or self-doubt crops up.

Write out your answers or find some other way of documenting your experience. (We also have a worksheet for this exercise available to download at http://www.yourcourageouslife.com /courage-habit, where you'll find a whole host of other resources that complement the work you're doing in this book.) Another option is to discuss these questions with a friend, asking her to reflect to you what she's noticed you doing in your life.

1. What's a dream that you've long held or a life change you've wanted to make that hasn't happened yet? Write down what you've wanted, and, as you write it down, describe it with a bit of detail. Instead of writing "travel the world" or "put up healthy boundaries with my family," write down *everything* you can think of about why that dream of traveling the world would be so great. Or, write down everything you'd be capable of if you managed to enact healthy boundaries with your family.

2. When you tell yourself why you haven't made that dream or life change happen, what reasons do you give? Beyond not having enough time or money, why hasn't it happened? List all the reasons.

3. In what situations do you notice yourself comparing yourself to others, and what exactly are the comparisons? (For example, "It happens at work. There's this other woman who seems like she's more creative and has better ideas." Or, "Our neighbor down the street has three kids and always seems much more on top of things as a mother than I am even though I only have one kid.")

4. Consider how fear stops you in any type of process. How does fear stop you before you can really start?

Or, when have you managed to get going and then fear swoops in and overwhelms you?

5. Finish this sentence five different ways: "I feel like I'm not good enough when…"

When you're finished answering the questions, scan your answers and look for anything repetitive, such as things that you tend to think and say, or circumstances that are chronic. For instance, is there one thought that keeps coming up, over and over? (For example, "I'm always deciding that it's not the right time.") Is there something that you seem to always tell yourself? (For example, "Whether I'm psyching myself out or feeling like I'm not good enough, I always think: 'Why bother trying?'") Are there any circumstances that you can identify that seem to come up, again and again? (For example, "Each time that I've started and then not followed through, it was because I felt the pinch of not having enough money and decided that I had to stop going after my passion and start making more money.")

Make sure that you identify three specific fears and write them down. As you complete different exercises in the chapters to come, you'll apply the exercises to these specific fears, so that by the time you finish the book those fears don't carry the same weight.

Please be gentle with yourself during this process. It's tough to look so closely at what we fear. This process isn't about getting rid of fear, since that's impossible. You're going to need to go *into* the fear and look at it clearly. You won't make courage into a habit by flipping a switch. That's just not how change happens. Gentleness with yourself and with your process is necessary and will get you where you want to go.

Four Common Fear Routines

I've heard many people share about their experiences of fear, and almost everyone worries at least a little bit that their experiences are so unique they can't be helped. However, I've found that there are four fear routines that are the most common: I call them the Perfectionist, the Saboteur, the Martyr, and the Pessimist. I break down each of these common fear routines below, outlining what we typically think, say, and do when we're stuck in them.

While you can find aspects of yourself in all these routines, one is usually the predominant routine that you turn to most often, and that's what I'll ask you to consider as you read through the description of each routine. Getting clear on the fear routine that you're most likely to turn to will help you to see the routine fully and with presence. If you understand your fear routine, it's harder for that routine to be repeated unconsciously.

The Perfectionist Routine

The Perfectionist routine is ruled by the drive to do it better. There's a chronic dissatisfaction with results, which sometimes makes the Perfectionist critique everything around her, feeling irritated and unable to go with the flow of life because it's not perfect. People caught in the Perfectionist routine often finds themselves overperforming in multiple areas of their lives and hiding imperfections while pretending that everything is okay. Perfectionists will do more than their fair share to look good or receive external approval. Or, because they don't trust that someone else will do it according to their own standards, they sometimes overwhelm themselves by setting impossibly high standards.

Perfectionists will frequently find themselves thinking about their own internal critiques of how they should have done something better or how others should have done it better. Perfectionists might say to themselves: "Why didn't you catch that mistake; it was so obvious," or, "What's the point of having them do it, if they can't do it right?" When things happen that are outside of their control, they'll either turn the blame outward, criticizing others, or inward, criticizing themselves. They consistently take on way too much, feel overwhelmed and exhausted, or treat being busy like a "high" where it "feels good" to tick things off the to-do list. The high always has a lull, however, at which point there is exhaustion, resentment about the built-up obligations, or a feeling that fun always comes last. People stuck in this routine tend to seem like they have no problems and a great life. Inwardly, they often feel tired, angry, or like they don't really know who they are or what they want.

Other Perfectionist routine behaviors may be nitpicking about small issues or getting disproportionately upset about small things, over-working, trying to control, and judging others or themselves. The judgment can vacillate between thinking they are better than others or silently comparing and considering themselves to be not good enough. They might judge others by saying to themselves: "I mean, why can't she get it together?" Sometimes, these behaviors can turn into a "mean girls'" syndrome, complete with competition, jealousy, and undermining others' accomplishments. Because approval fuels this routine, the "reward" of being praised by coworkers or others makes it difficult to see the benefit of unhooking from a constant cycle of doing. Perfectionists can have trouble telling the difference between the kind of high standards that help them live a better life versus the kind of high standards that are exhausting to maintain.

The Saboteur

The hallmark of the Saboteur routine is an inability to make sustained progress due to a pattern of taking two steps forward and one step back. People who are stuck in the Saboteur routine find themselves constantly bouncing from thing to thing, having difficulty with commitment. Perhaps they'll feel excited about something and then quickly feel tied down by that very thing so that it feels like an obligation. They get feedback from others about not really "applying" themselves. The Saboteur also tends to change homes, jobs, and relationships frequently. Some would call this the "shiny object syndrome," which refers to people who are always being seduced by the next big thing or the thing that looks better. They have difficulties with accountability, finishing what they start, and not getting enough traction or movement to sustain something. They jump into projects without getting foundational aspects in place because it's either too much work or kills the creative spontaneity. They tend to stop trying as soon as something no longer holds their interest. They can create chaos to overwhelm themselves so that they don't need to take action.

Someone stuck in the Saboteur routine is thinking about how to avoid or get out of commitments that are often connected to something that they initially felt excited about or were interested in, but aren't anymore. They tell themselves things such as, "Well, I got at least a little bit done, so now I can take a break." While we all need downtime, people caught in the Saboteur routine start doing things that reverse or undermine progress they've already made. They'll spend because they saved, binge on unhealthy foods because they exercised, or take on too much right when they were starting to get some momentum going. They get irritated with people who try to hold them accountable. To justify not really putting sustained effort in the direction of their dreams, you may hear them say phrases to themselves such as: "This person [who wants me to be accountable] is being way too rigid and they need to relax! I'll get it done in my own time!" They feel controlled by commitments, and are most likely to use phrases such as "I'm going to live by my own rules!" or "I need ease and self-care" to justify not really putting sustained effort in the direction of their dreams.

Other examples of Saboteur behaviors include putting forth tiny efforts and expecting big returns, waiting until the last possible minute to deal with something uncomfortable, getting upset with others who expect them to follow through on what they say they're going to do, or failing to take the time to put things into place for long-term success. Saboteurs trying to unhook from this routine often find themselves struggling to rely on their instincts. Or, they may have a hard time telling the difference between quitting something because it's not right for them versus quitting something because the routine has hooked them, again.

The Martyr Routine

You know a Martyr routine when you see people who are relentless in their self-sacrifice and people pleasing. They've let their lives focus so much on service to others that they don't make time for their own dreams and desires. They use their self-imposed obligations to others as a reason why the things they might want for themselves are impossible to attain. Someone playing out the Martyr routine might even enable others by stepping in with money or other resources for adult children or friends who are perfectly capable of taking care of themselves, or with people who need to suffer the consequences of their own behavior. For example, a parent who steps in to provide his adult child a place to live after she has gone on a credit card spending spree and can't pay her rent would be considered a Martyr. Martyrs justify this sort of behavior by telling themselves "What else could I do? I had to step in. No one else can love or nurture or be there for them like I can." They overwhelm themselves by stockpiling obligations they feel to everyone else, leaving no time for their own desires.

People stuck in a Martyr routine are probably secretly hoping to be noticed for their good deeds and selflessness, to get credit for what they've sacrificed, or to be validated by others. They think that it's their job to protect people from the consequences of their poor decisions. When they put more attention on someone else's needs, they tell themselves things like "I couldn't take time for myself just then—someone else needed me," or, "I had to step in, or else they'd suffer." (In other words, someone would experience the natural consequence of their own poor choices.) Other times, Martyrs tell themselves that they couldn't handle the impact of someone being mad at them, and that's why they had to caretake.

Other examples of Martyr behaviors include saying yes even when one really wants to say no, people pleasing, and excessively worrying about what others think. Martyrs might get upset (usually a low-grade resentment) when others don't notice or give them credit for what they do, at which point they'll feel taken for granted. They tend to be self-sacrificing to a fault, such as the mom who won't schedule a necessary doctor's appointment for herself because it conflicts with her son's weekly lesson that could easily be skipped or rescheduled. Or, they might let everyone else make the decisions, but then say, "Well, everyone else wanted something different, so I didn't feel like I could change our plans." Martyrs who start to unhook from this routine often notice themselves feeling confused about the difference between acts of kindness for others, and the sort of self-sacrifice that depletes them.

The Pessimist Routine

While Martyrs tend to think the things they want aren't possible because of their self-imposed obligations to other people, someone stuck in a Pessimist routine fundamentally believes that things won't work out because things just don't work out *for them.* This then becomes the reason not to act or take responsibility.

A typical phrase a Pessimist might say when considering new possibilities is: "It'd be nice, but it'll never happen." If you ask someone stuck in a Pessimist headspace what she'd like to be different, you're likely to be met with sarcasm: "Well, it'd be great if I didn't have to have a job and could just lie around a pool all day. I'm *sure* that's going to happen right after I win the lottery, huh?" Or, the person won't even engage with the question: "What's the point of saying what I want? It's not like I have the time."

People stuck in a Pessimist routine will insist that it's just not possible to change something, and that the opportunities for change simply aren't there. They may get irritated with anyone who suggests otherwise or brings up legitimate solutions to problems. Pessimists insist on their own incapability, even when the capability is there. There is a kind of futile hopelessness in relationship to their dreams. It's not clinical depression, but more like a shrug of the shoulders at the idea that some big, bold dream could be theirs. ("Sure, it'd be nice, but who would pay the bills?") Other times, the Pessimist routine will show up as a refusal to say sorry or admit to doing anything wrong, because the Pessimist is busy noticing how she was done wrong by someone else.

Someone stuck in a Pessimist routine sees the world through a lens of doubt, and is often consumed with all the ways that something is unfair or the ways that so-and-so with power is trying to screw over someone else. (For example, the person may think that his mother-in-law is trying to screw over the family; the utility companies are trying to screw over their customers with the bills; or the teacher is trying to screw over his kid). While issues of systemic oppression are real, when people are caught in a Pessimist routine, they aren't thinking about these things from the place of how to give voice to the larger scope of social injustices or to change something. They are only focused on how life has singled them out personally to suffer, and they are insistent that they can't do anything about it even when options are presented or available. Pessimists might find themselves saying things such as "If I didn't watch out for myself, it's not like anyone else would," or "Even though I do my best, it never works out for me," or "Why bother? Nothing will change." Sometimes, the routine is taken out on others around them: "You never do this [thing that you should be doing], and I always have to do this [thing that I don't want to do, as a result]."

Other examples of Pessimist behaviors include feeling low-grade resentment or anger without really doing anything about the problem, sending passive-aggressive emails or making passive-aggressive comments, pointing out various ways that someone else did it wrong with no ownership for one's own mistakes, or pointing out various ways that something should be changed but not taking action to change it. (For example, they may hate their job but don't do anything to change jobs, and there's always a reason. "I'd never find another job! There's no money, there's not time." Then, if a job opportunity becomes available, there's another reason: "Well, it's not the right time," or, "Well, but there would be a commute.")

Someone trying to get out of the Pessimist routine often finds herself struggling to see possibility and what she's capable of creating even if circumstances such as lack of money or time are factors.

Which routine is your predominant one? First, take some time to get clear on which routine is your go-to. Again, it's great to notice when pieces of other routines apply. We don't always fit into just one routine. Sometimes we experience fear differently depending on the context. In one scenario where you feel "not good enough," you might turn to the Perfectionist routine, which runs on striving and proving behaviors. When that becomes exhausting, you might turn to the Saboteur routine, which tells you to run in the complete opposite direction: "Take it easy; don't worry about this right now." With your family, you might be more of a Martyr, and with your job you might go into more of a Pessimist headspace.

Moving Forward

Things get exciting once people know what their fear routines are. I realize that "exciting" might not be the first word that comes to mind for you, but bear with me. Things get exciting at this juncture because now you've got some essential pieces in place for embarking on this journey. Knowing which fear routine you default to gives you the power to stop living on autopilot from a fear-based place, and to start untangling yourself from the overall "fear pattern" of cue-routine-reward. Life will always have its cues, but if you can shift the "routine" part of the cue-routine-reward pattern, then you can shift the entire pattern itself. Imagine how life would be if you started moving in the direction of your most courageous self, noticed an old routine such as the Martyr or Perfectionist, and found that you could do things differently? This is where things have immense power to change for the better.

In the chapters that follow, you'll learn how to implement each part in the Courage Habit process and bring forth that most courageous self that you defined in Chapter 1. You'll be examining your own fear routines and applying each step of the Courage Habit so that your fear routine can't function in the way that it's accustomed to. The shift awaits you! Get ready—things are going to change, and it's going to be brilliant!

Chapter 3

Accessing the Body

In movies and on television, we usually see people making a big decision, perhaps to be with the one they love or to never again tolerate someone else's mistreatment, and then they just…take action. They *know* better, so they immediately start *doing* better. They follow their heart or make the big declaration, and then they logically move straight past whatever doubt had been holding them back before.

Should be simple, right? Nope. Fear isn't logical and change is a process. Our old patterns can play out unconsciously, even when we "know better." For instance, in the Introduction, I shared how I knew that I wanted to leave my job, yet, during periods of uncertainty, I'd find myself craving a little hit of the familiar, such as the validation I'd get from colleagues. To make myself feel better I'd take on extra work, which was a distraction from spending time on creating my new path. We don't abandon old ways of being overnight. Our basal ganglia and the pull of the cue-routine-reward loop will take some time to unwire. We can logically know that we want to shift into living the way our most courageous self would live, yet the *feeling* of fear in the body can be so paralyzing that we go right back to choosing the things that don't work but that are known and familiar. That's why knowing what the sensations of fear are like for you is so helpful. When you tune in to the fact that fear exists and shows up as a sensation in your body, it gives you the power to get present and recognize when fear is there. To change the fear routine, you've got to get present to the feeling of fear and have ways of handling what you feel, which is why the first step in the Courage Habit is something I call "accessing the body."

My first foray into accessing the body was during that Christmas break when I tuned in to my body and realized that the low-grade feeling of discomfort I'd been feeling was, to my surprise, fear. But, I didn't learn about the power of accessing the body as a regular practice until I stayed at the Green Gulch Zen Center, located in a remote valley in Marin County, just outside of San Francisco. At the time, I had picked Green Gulch for practical reasons: I needed a weekend away, it was quiet, and there was no Wi-Fi that would tempt me into yet another work-related email check. I had no interest in meditation, because it made me feel vaguely nuts, as if every critical voice in my head collectively decided to start talking at once. However, I decided that while I was at Green Gulch, I'd be a good sport and give meditation another shot.

To my surprise, when I sat down during the first day's meditation session, I didn't just relax. The longer I sat, the more I could think clearly. My shoulders fell. I could breathe deeper. The more that I performed the simple act of sitting and breathing, it was obvious that anything I'd thought was a huge problem was something I was completely capable of handling if I took it piece by piece. In other words, slowing down to breathe took me out of fear, worry, and doubt, and into feeling like I could handle what arose.

I know, I know…this is what everyone says about meditation, mindfulness, and stillness practices. You start by trying to relieve a little stress, and then the next thing you know, you're writing self-help books about courage and talking about things like *wanting to get present*. But, I was hooked! After that first revelatory experience, I attended all Green Gulch's daily practice sessions throughout the duration of my stay. The only way to describe the experience I had in that first session would be to say that the stillness I'd longed for crept inside my heart and took up residence, letting me know that it was there any time I needed it. The more I meditated, the more I felt calm, clear, and aligned with my most courageous self.

I realize that there is an element of this that sounds rote and goody-two-shoes. Meditate? We've all heard it before, but I can't underscore enough how important a body-based practice is to aid you in stopping the sensations of fear from getting you stuck. After that weekend, I had the first tool for stopping those auto-pilot, basal ganglia impulses from taking over. The hardest part of changing an emotionally based habit is not realizing that the habit is occurring. When we regularly practice body-based tools, we have the ability to get present with those automatic processes so they can be examined. When I began to regularly take the time to slow down and breathe on the job, during difficult conversations, or at any moment I was about to back down from taking action to change my life, I was able to notice fear sensations before I went into my Perfectionist routine. This is the critical process that will empower you to stop the same cycle from repeating itself.

Practices like meditation often call for a particular kind of attention to experience known as *mindfulness*. It's about slowing down to become aware of the present moment—everything you feel in your body and all the thoughts crossing through your mind—and just noticing it all, without judging. Mindfulness-based practices help you to access the body to work through challenging moments with presence.

Accessing the body isn't woo-woo; it's a completely practical, research-backed tool. The research into the benefits of any kind of practice to slow down and breathe are numerous. Many of them confirm that you don't need to adopt a formal meditation practice to learn how to access your body, nor do you need to find a guru, go to a Zen center, or create a ritual. You just need simple ways of accessing your body that will give you the power to pause before fear gets too heightened and before your fear routine is harder to control. In this chapter, you'll learn simple ways to slow down and how to use your body to work through feelings of fear and practice courage.

You Can't Logic Your Way Through

Chances are good that when it comes to facing your fears, you've already tried talking yourself out of feeling afraid with strategies such as reminding yourself that "worst-case scenarios rarely happen." Or, perhaps you've tried the extremes of completely ignoring those fearful voices, or internally shouting down any fears, telling them to shut up and quit bothering you. Confession time: I've tried all these strategies, so if you're recognizing yourself here, you're not alone.

The thing is, in the short term, these strategies *can* have some efficacy, which makes us think that they're workable strategies when there's a temporary decrease in stress and we feel that hit of "reward" in the cue-routine-reward cycle. However, in the long term, trying to logic your way through fear doesn't work. That's because fear isn't logical; it's primal.

Why doesn't it work to logic your way through fear? Using logic is an attempt to control the cue, the fear itself, rather than change the routine. In the moments when we use logic to try to stop our fear, we're hoping that ignoring fear, telling self-doubt to take a hike, or talking ourselves out of what we feel will keep the fear from truly registering. We think if we find a way to dismiss the fear early on, we won't really need to deal with it. It's a way of trying to avoid the cue of fear altogether.

Unfortunately, no one can arrange their lives in such a way that those fear cues never happen. This is life! It gets messy, and everyone experiences challenges. The most healthy, well-adjusted people on the planet with robust self-esteem experience fear and moments of self-doubt. We're human beings having a human experience, and we feel fear in our bodies, not just our heads.

The bottom line is that we can't inoculate ourselves from uncomfortable, challenging, fearful, or uncertain situations in life, and we're not supposed to. A sanitized life might be predictable, but it's not much fun. It's not the life your most courageous self would want. Since fear is going to come up, let's find ways to work through it. Consciously choosing to access the body is a powerful tool for getting present and clear right in the moment when you're about to go into a fear routine by default. The mindfulness-based practices you'll learn in this chapter will lessen the impact of fear sensations in your body and bring you to clearer thinking about your next, most courageous move.

Janelle

Janelle is a mother of three, and during our very first session when I asked her why she wanted to start coaching, she joked, "It's the only way I'm going to get to have an adult conversation during the day!" Her oldest two children were in school, and she was home the rest of the time with her two-year-old son while her husband was at work. A babysitter came once every other week to watch Janelle's two-year-old son for the afternoon. As she shared that she was combining power walking with our coaching call, I quickly learned that Janelle was the queen of multitasking.

As our light chatter gave way to me asking what she specifically wanted to focus on, I heard her voice shift and the tears came, suddenly. "I'm always snapping at my kids," she said, breathing heavily as she tried to stop crying. "Every single day I wake up and I tell myself that I'm going to stop. But, within an hour of my husband leaving for work, I'm doing it again. I'm getting irritated at the chaos of trying to get out the door to school, how they fight, or mess up some drawer that I just got organized. I feel short-tempered with my youngest, most days. And, then I'm so pissed at myself afterward!"

"Where are you, right now?" I asked her. "Can you sit down on a bench for a moment?" I felt as if I could also feel the weight that Janelle was carrying, struggling with how to manage the needs of three different children and how much she was judging herself for not doing it the way she had mapped it out in her head. To my surprise, however, Janelle's voice shifted again, but this time she was quickly collecting herself.

"No," she said, "I just don't have the time. I need to get my workout in. I don't want to spend the babysitter money and not get everything done that I need to get done within this hour. I just need some strategies for managing my feelings of being overwhelmed."

Janelle's desires to hurry up and get to the strategy, the to-do list of action items for her problems, were understandable. After all, being a mother of three isn't a walk in the park. Yet, I had to deliver some bad news. "My approach might be a bit slower than that," I said. "But I think that if we take the time to fully see what's going on, there are some specific actions you can take that will help. Does that work?"

Janelle agreed to try, which I knew was a start. As we talked about how she felt in her day-to-day life, I suspected that part of the reason she felt overwhelmed and irritated was because her feelings were seeking an outlet. Paradoxically, if she kept trying to clamp down on her feelings and hide them, the pressure for release would build and those feelings would keep "leaking out" in small ways, such as snapping at her children.

"Who would you be and what kind of life would you be living if you weren't overwhelmed?" I asked her, wanting to initiate a conversation that might guide Janelle toward articulating what her most courageous self would look like.

"I'd be the relaxed, chill mom," Janelle said, and then she laughed. "That sounds kind of stupid."

"Nope. It sounds like the desire of every mom I've ever talked to, including myself," I said, laughing with her. "Let's dig deeper. Who would you be if you were the 'relaxed, chill mom'?"

"I'd be…I guess I'd be who I thought I was always going to be before I ever got pregnant. I used to work for a 'grants for the arts' initiative. I'd get these free tickets to different shows because it was my job to check out the art before we'd approve the grant, and I was connected to all these different artistic subcultures, and we'd talk about art all day," Janelle said, lightness entering her voice again. "I thought I'd be different than the other moms who freaked out about every little thing. I thought I'd just strap a baby in a body wrap and walk around a gallery with a glass of wine and people would coo and I'd do the mom-plus-work thing. But, once I had the first child, I was too tired to go back to work. Then I got pregnant with my second child so quickly, and my husband was laid off for a while after my second was born. It would have been impossible to afford daycare, so I quit. Then, we decided to have a third child, and my husband is working again, but I've never thought about going back to work."

"Really?" I asked, surprised. "You've never thought, at all, about going back?" Janelle puffed as she walked, and I waited an uncomfortably long time. Finally, when she spoke, I could hear her fighting back emotion again.

"I think about it all of the time, actually. What I mean is that I just never think that it's a possibility to go back."

"Okay, then—do you *want* to go back?" I asked.

"No, of course not," Janelle said immediately. "Who else would step in? I don't know how I'd get everything done if I was also working. Someone has to run the house, you know. Match the socks. Remember to buy the vegetables that my kids won't eat anyway. Not that anyone notices. And, I don't know how I'd deal with the stress of a job again."

As we kept trying to clarify what her most courageous self would want, Janelle kept pivoting back to her desires to be a great mom. Of course, it made sense that being a great mom was important to her, but there was something about how she kept turning back to "being a great mom" repeatedly. What was *outside* of that role? Even when Janelle talked about how nice it would be to go to art shows again, just for fun, she'd immediately add that she couldn't take time away from her children.

As I considered Janelle's process, I could see the beginnings of her cue-routine-reward cycle emerging. The cue was the pressure and overwhelm of trying to be a fully dedicated, twenty-four-seven mom. She tried to clamp down on the cue by using logic and reaching for strategies to manage her feelings of being overwhelmed, but it wasn't a long-term solution. The routine entered the picture when the overwhelmness (fear, self-doubt, and stress) all got to be too much, and she snapped at her kids. Snapping at her kids brought momentary relief but was immediately followed by guilt. I asked Janelle to tell me more about the guilt.

"The guilt comes on pretty quickly," Janelle said, "But, there's this moment where, right after I shout, my kids actually freaking *listen to me* for five seconds. They stop whining or fighting with each other, and they get really quiet because, you know, 'Mom's mad, we'd better behave.'"

"So, if we're going to shift this, we're going to need to interrupt the cue-routine-reward cycle," I said. "And, I think I might even have some 'strategy' for you if you're interested."

"Oooh, strategy! You've won me over. Tell me more," Janelle said, lightness coming back into her voice.

"We start by using a tool—a 'strategy' you might prefer to call it—called accessing the body. There are lots of ways to access the body. You can dance, stretch, run, meditate, or whatever you want, but I usually recommend just taking a few minutes to breathe, and notice any insights that arise."

Janelle was quiet for a moment, and I wasn't sure if she was mulling it over or thinking that I was just some new age life coach. "For what it's worth," I added, selling it a bit, "There's a ton of research, all legit, backing the idea that this approach is helpful."

"Alright, I'll try it," Janelle said, "But only because you didn't suggest buying a sage stick."

"Well, I always wait until I've worked with someone for a few months before I start talking about sage sticks," I joked back.

Jokes aside, my hope was that accessing the body would be a first step to help Janelle feel more patient with herself and her kids, as well as provide her with some insights into what she really wanted for her life, beyond being a mother. If she was stuck in being overwhelmed, it was going to be difficult for her to do anything except repeat the same cycles that she'd been spinning in.

The Body Scan

Accessing the body is the key for noticing fear where it starts. Remember Eliana who was completing her MBA while working full-time, juggling the stress of being the only woman on her team, and getting so caught up in the details that she ended up getting even less accomplished? It was identifying that fear sensation of urgency that helped her to see the moment when she was about to get off track. In Chapter 2, you were also asked to think about your own fear sensations and how they showed up in your body. Revisit naming those sensations now. When fear, self-doubt, hesitation, or worry arise for you, does it show up as a tight throat? Inability to concentrate? Irritation? Sweaty palms?

Try thinking about some of those fear sensations that you identified, and then taking a moment to simply breathe. What do you notice? This simple moment to breathe is all you need, to start.

Janelle started with taking some time to simply breathe to access her body, and later we talked about how to do a more in-depth practice for accessing the body: a body scan. In working with clients, I've found that a body scan is the simplest and most straightforward way to access the body because it can be done anytime and anywhere, and it takes less than five minutes.

It works like this: Start at your feet. Ask your feet, "Hey, what's up today? No pressure. Just curious." The lightness of this approach is intentional, because the simpler this practice is, the easier it is to utilize. Of course, if you prefer a different question, that's totally fine. Some of my clients have customized this practice for themselves with questions such as "What would you like me to know?" or "What feels true?" Then, move to your knees. Ask your knees your question: "Hey, what's up today? No pressure. Just curious." Move to your thighs. Given that women receive so much negative conditioning around their weight, this can be an area where it feels harder to relax and remain unattached, but see what you can notice. "Hey, what's up today? No pressure. Just curious." Move to your pelvis. "Hey, what's up today?" Then to your stomach: "Hey, what's up today? No pressure. Just curious." From there, move to your chest, shoulders, neck, and forehead, asking each one the same question: "Hey, what's up today?"

Take a moment to try out this process. Set the timer on your phone or stove for just three to five minutes, breathe a bit, and see what happens. Allow yourself to get curious about what you notice. There's no need to try to change it; this is just about noticing. You might feel any number of sensations when you're doing a body scan, and translate those sensations to a wide number of emotions: curiosity, calm, nervousness, and even happiness. To help clients better see the cue-routine-reward process as it applies to fear patterns, I try to help them also recognize sensations that might specifically be tied to fear. The following are the most common:

- A churning sensation in the gut accompanied by the thought "Something doesn't feel right."

- A tight feeling anywhere in the body. (Take deep breaths when you encounter this feeling; it indicates something's up.)

- An inability to concentrate or focus.

- A feeling of being a "deer in headlights," suddenly unable to gather your thoughts or articulate a response.

- A sense that some sensation is arising, but one you can't quite gather the words to describe.

When fear sensations arise, you're probably going to want to shut them down, disassociate, or distract yourself by thinking about something else. I'll help you to learn how to "set a container" around those feelings later in this chapter. For now, I only want to make the point that the more you are willing to sit with feelings of fear in the body during a short exercise, the more you train yourself to sit with fear when you're taking the bold, daring risks you identified as part of your path to your most courageous self. If you'd like some help completing the Body Scan exericse, visit http://www.yourcourageouslife.com/courage-habit for a guided meditation.

The body scan I'm suggesting here is just one way of accessing the body. It's not necessarily the only way, or even what will ultimately be your way. The point, again, is to find some way of accessing the body so that when fear-based sensations arise, you can feel them without being pulled into an old fear routine, and you can instead continue in the direction of your deepest desires.

If the body scan's just not working for you after trying it for a while, or if you want to try some other way of getting in touch with your body and what it feels, there are other options.

- Try asking the different parts of your body something like "What do you need?" or "What would you like me to know?" and seeing if any different answers arise.

- Dance. Turn on Spotify, YouTube, or Pandora if you don't already have a favorite playlist saved somewhere. Set the music to random and dance at home, on your own. Choose different styles of songs for different days. On one day, James Brown might make you feel vibrant and badass. On another day, Dustin O'Halloran's Quartet No. 2 might bring up tears. On another day, a Chopin piano sonata might leave you feeling contemplative. Move your body to the beat of whatever you put on.

- Run. Some people hate running because it's so difficult. I love it because it's so difficult that my brain stops chattering and my total focus and presence goes to my body and breath. Yours might, too.

- Yoga. If you've ever felt like yoga wasn't your thing, keep searching. There are so many different styles of yoga, and even within one style there are different teachers that each add their own flavor. I was a haphazard yoga attendee until I discovered Vinyasa flow. My best friend, Valerie, loves a slow, methodical Iyengar class. Another friend of mine is into super-steamy Bikram yoga.

- Stretching. Who says it needs to be yoga? Sit on your floor in comfortable clothes and stretch your legs. Make circles with your ankles. Reach your arms above your head. Breathe.

- Sex or self-pleasure. If it's mindful, and if you're accessing the body while doing it, it counts. Enjoy!

- Hiking or walking. Choose a trail or pick your pavement. Walk for a set amount of time just while continuously coming back to your breath and noticing what's happening in your body.

- Visualization. Close your eyes and imagine yourself radiant and happy. Picture your life with vivid detail, doing work that you love, glowing with health, connected to the best of friends, in love with your partner, and more.

Whatever you do, keep your approach to accessing the body small and doable, and take as few as five minutes to do it. Pay attention to what you feel and what comes up, and jot down a few notes. As Janelle would soon find, even with a rough start, accessing the body over time brings the most insight.

Accessing the Body for Insights

After a few weeks of working together, Janelle had solidified a few critical pieces of the coaching process. She'd determined that her Primary Focus included "go to art shows" and "feel like a relaxed mom." I still had my own ideas that there could be more to the picture, but I knew that even defining that much and fitting in time for our sessions was a lot for Janelle. We'd also determined her primary fear routine was the Martyr. "Guilty as charged," Janelle had said, the day that we talked about that routine. "As it happens, my son freaked out when I tried to leave for my walk-and-talk with you, so guess who caved and put him in the stroller while the babysitter sits at home?"

There was just one area where things weren't going well: accessing the body. Body scans, Janelle said, were a total flop.

They gave her *more* stress, not less. She hated feeling uncomfortable fear sensations arise, even though she logically understood that if she wasn't willing to work through them, things weren't going to change anytime soon. "Instead of relaxing, I just feel more upset," she reported after another week during which she had felt resistant to any kind of body-based practice between sessions. "I get this feeling in the pit of my stomach, and then I feel annoyed that I'm using what little time I have each day to do some breathing exercise when there are fifteen things around the house that need to be picked up."

I was glad that Janelle was bringing up her objections so honestly. I wouldn't have wanted to keep doing something that was making me feel more stressed, rather than less, either! Yet, I also knew that everyone wants to avoid this part of working through their fear—the part where they need to feel it, instead of avoiding it. This is always a challenging moment when I'm helping someone examine their fears, because we've got to navigate that fine line between forcing and rushing the process. And, we don't want to avoid the process simply because it's uncomfortable. I asked Janelle if she felt open to trying some work to access the body right there on the phone, in a more supported, guided way, and she agreed.

"Give that feeling, that sensation in your stomach, a voice. What does it say?" I asked. What Janelle shared next became the insight that would inform our coaching work in the coming months. It unraveled a cycle of stress that had felt impossible to get out of since she became a mother, and became the catalyst for her to reclaim the work in the art world that she had loved doing and had missed for so many years.

Janelle took a deep breath. "It says, 'You're not being a good mother.'" *You're not being a good mother.* That was the fear that

Janelle hadn't wanted to look at. This fear was running behind the scenes, driving her to be ever-more self-sacrificing through a Martyr routine, and it was wearing her down. If she avoided accessing the body, there was no need to feel that fear and discomfort of worrying that maybe she wasn't being a good mother.

"Let's unpack that a bit," I suggested. "What do good mothers do, in your estimation?" Janelle rattled off a list of things she was constantly juggling: taking her children to lessons and sports practices, negotiating their disagreements, trying to keep the house clean, giving them all their one-on-one time, meal planning, shopping, and more. She felt driven by the idea that she needed to be a good mother, and simultaneously resentful of those demands, but admitting to her feelings of resentment felt difficult to do.

"Sometimes I even think to myself, 'Have the kids had the right balance of social time and independent play?' So, when I'm not upset with myself for not spending enough time with them, I worry that they aren't getting the right amount of time to play on their own," she told me. Janelle was starting to see how the fear of not being a good mom had her rushing to overcompensate. She was trying save her kids from any feelings of disappointment by handling everything for them. Even though she logically knew that this wasn't going to do them any good in the long term, the fear of not being a good mother frequently compelled her to step in, make suggestions, or interrupt their play just to see if they needed her. Sometimes she found that she didn't even notice that she had stepped in, until she had finished straightening a room that she had asked her two oldest children to pick up themselves. Why was she doing this? Some of it was social conditioning that places a high price on what it means to be considered a "good mother." Some of it was how Janelle was raised and the model of motherhood that she grew up with. And, some of it was Janelle's own Martyr tendencies, which predated her life as a mother.

"That's why some kind of practice with the body can be helpful to you," I said. "Getting present with the body is what's going to help you notice that moment when you're compelled to step in with the Martyr routine, before you actually go into it all the way."

Janelle decided to get serious about practicing accessing the body. At first, she was just slowing down enough to notice what was happening, recognizing her fear sensations and the impulses that were tied to them to intervene with her kids. Later, as she began holding herself back from constantly micromanaging, she practiced accessing the body to make it through the moments when her children were adjusting to the new mother that was emerging. This new mother didn't so readily clean up their messes or give them what they wanted.

Pausing to breathe kept Janelle from moving on autopilot as a mother, and as she began clearing away some of the overwhelmness, she asked herself what she *really* wanted beyond being a mother. That's when she was ready to take those first steps to get back into the art world and go to art-related events. Doing those things for herself made her feel calmer and more patient. She also discovered cracks in her marriage that she hadn't wanted to look at. Throwing herself into her role as a mother had been a distraction from that. Janelle used "accessing the body" to navigate the tough, honest conversations that she'd needed to have with her husband about the division of responsibility in their home, how they wanted to parent, and how they could reconnect as a couple. It was bumpy for a while, but the entire family arrived at a better place as Janelle reconnected with who she is and translated that to how she lived in her daily life.

At the start of working together, Janelle's cue-routine-reward loop looked like this:

Cue: The demands of parenting in self-sacrificing ways that met social expectation and the feeling of being overwhelmed that came with it. The fear of not being a good mother, which was particularly aroused any time Janelle allowed herself to think of pursuing her own interests.

Routine (Martyr): Janelle went into this routine on autopilot, and it helped her avoid stepping into what she truly wanted—to reconnect with her own creative passions and reenter the workforce.

Reward: A short-term decrease in anxiety, but in the long term the return of feeling overwhelmed, and a sense she wasn't living a life that she was authentically excited about.

After working together for a few months, her cue-routine-reward loop looked more like this:

Cue: The demands of parenting and feeling overwhelmed, and the fears of not being a good mother.

Routine: Janelle's new routine was developing based on the steps of the Courage Habit. She would access the body so that she could slow down and really get to know what she was feeling. Later, she would add in the other Courage Habit steps by listening to what her fear said but without getting attached to it, then reframing the limiting fear-based Stories: *I won't be a good mother if I work; It's selfish if I choose to be a working mom* and *My husband and* *the kids need me too much.* She also started forming more connections with other moms and reaching out for help if she needed it.

Reward: Feeling less overwhelmed and more capable of noticing the fear sensations that propelled her Martyr routine. This allowed her to stop going into that fear routine and to start making choices that were more aligned with what she really wanted for her life.

Putting a Container Around the Experience

Note that when Janelle began to engage with accessing the body, she initially disliked the process because it was bringing up things she'd rather ignore, and it wasn't taking her straight to answers. This is a very common experience. Who wants to do something that initially brings up things that are uncomfortable? Others resist this practice because they're worried that they will run up against strong emotions if they do a body scan. If you realize that you're sad, mad, or that life in general sucks after checking in with your body, what do you do with those strong emotions? Hanging out in negative states for long periods of time will only drain you. So, what else is there?

This is where I usually introduce the concept of "putting a container around the experience." Imagine that there's a container and within that container things are messy, but because the walls of the container are there, the mess doesn't spill outside creating hazards elsewhere. This concept is about giving yourself the space you need to feel the raw truth of what you feel and the boundaries you need to keep those feelings from taking over. Here are just a few examples of ways to "put a container around" the experience of accessing the body if you're worried about strong emotions coming up:

- Set a timer in another room so that you'll need to interrupt what you're feeling to turn it off when it starts to ring. This creates the space to be fully with any negative sensations that arise, with the security of knowing that there will be an interruption prompting you not to spend too much time in that space.

- Tell a friend what you're doing, and text this person asking him or her to call you at a set time. The phone call is the interruption, and it can also become a check-in on how you're feeling.

- Find a friend who would work well as a "venting partner." A venting partner is just as it sounds—a designated person who will hold space for you while you're venting. They'll listen if you need to yell, cry, or get angry, with an agreement that whatever happens in the venting space isn't *who* you are, but rather purely an exercise for releasing feelings.

- Make a commitment to leave the house and take a walk immediately after accessing the body. Giving yourself something to do immediately afterward can help with any fears that the feelings will be too overwhelming.

- Work through exercises to access the body with a therapist, somatic counselor, or a coach who emphasizes body-based work.

Another thing to keep in mind is that while we often fear strong emotions, and that's why we resist body-based practices, they aren't the only ones that can come up! What if positive emotions are part of this process, and accessing the body is an uplifting experience? What if you found that you were incredibly joyful? Or ecstatic? Or grateful? What if you tried a body scan and realized that more than anything, you felt curious or sensual?

I'll never forget working with Lisa, who had always shied away from body-based practices because they brought up feelings of extreme sadness about her mother's death when she was a teenager. I understood why she was hesitant. Who wants to feel sadness and risk being caught there? Yet, I also knew that Lisa, just like the rest of us, had her own unique cue-routine-reward cycles that would run her if she didn't bring conscious awareness to the first fear cues that arose in her body.

"Well, what if you didn't need to cry to access the body?" I said, wanting to help Lisa find ways of engaging with an uncomfortable practice that put her in charge. "You know, you can create a practice like this in any way that you want. You're in the driver's seat. You could dance joyfully to one song a day. You could lay on the ground with your legs elevated and do some deep breathing. You could take one of your power walks. The important piece is that you pay attention to your body while you do it, and perhaps jot down a few thoughts afterward about what's coming up for you—that's it. Do any of those ideas resonate, for you?"

Lisa was drawn to the idea of dancing to one song daily and letting herself feel whatever arose organically during that song. She found that when she engaged with this practice, sometimes she would cry. But, because she had committed to only accessing the body for the length of one song, the end of a song became her "container" for an emotional space that would have otherwise felt too messy. Over time, she liked that she had this compartmentalized space for processing through old grief, and it wasn't a space that left her feeling worn out.

Most of us, when accessing the body, are like Lisa. We don't always have big *aha* moments about our lives when accessing the body, but we will find that when we use the practice regularly, small but meaningful insights rise to the surface. The practice of accessing the body makes us more aware of not going into old fear routines and fear feelings that might otherwise derail what we're trying to change.

No matter what strategy you use, putting a container around the experience of accessing the body and butting up against negative emotions is ultimately simple. You allow yourself to "get messy" within the container, cry if you want, drop the f-bomb, hit pillows, or whine and complain out loud to the walls of a room. However, you hold to the commitment of not going beyond the container. If your boundary is that when a timer goes off, the complaining stops, then be serious about it—the complaining stops. If your boundary is that after taking some time to access the body, you'll get out of the house and take a walk—take the walk.

With practice, you'll see for yourself that you can have a wide capacity for interacting with negative emotions if you set the right container. You don't need to avoid them. You don't need to squash them. There are boundaries that you can put in place that empower you to feel without difficult emotions spiraling into something bigger.

Remember, our fears tell us that accessing the body is going to be a purely negative experience that will overwhelm us, but that isn't so. Many of my clients have found that accessing the body puts them in touch with sides of themselves that are more playful, take themselves less seriously, or that are more in touch with their sensuality or femininity.

In this chapter, I pointed out that fear is not logical; it's primal and has the greatest impact on our lives when we feel it in our bodies. Joy isn't logical either; it's also primal and has the greatest impact on our lives when we feel it in our bodies. Your most courageous self may go on to *do* a lot of great, bold things, but you'll be happiest when you *feel* bold, *feel* courageous, and *feel* capable of creating the life you desire.

What's Next

Now that you know what's involved, what will you choose to practice when you access the body? If you wait to make a committed decision to use this tool, you're less likely to start taking action and accessing the body, and you won't get any further toward making your courageous life a reality. However, if you choose to access your body in some small way for just five minutes a day, you'll gain so many benefits. You'll come to recognize your fear and how it takes control, which gives you the knowledge you need to get present and make alternative choices.

There's also one other benefit that's central to the Courage Habit process: Accessing the body will create more room to start noticing what any inner, critical voices are saying, and how those voices tend to run unchecked. These are the internal voices that tell you things such as "You're not a good mother," "You're no good at this," or "People will think you're ridiculous if you try to change careers."

When I'm facing something in my life that intimidates me or feels vulnerable, that internal critic is usually harsh, loud, and condescending. Accessing the body slows down the nervous system so that the fear sensations don't accelerate, and that's when it's time to do something pro-active with those fear-based internal voices. In the next chapter, we'll explore the critical voice that stops you in your tracks right at the moment when change is most possible. Instead of trying to ignore that voice or get it to go away, you'll meet that voice and learn why it shows up and, most importantly, learn how to stop letting it have so much power.

Chapter 4

Listening Without Attachment

When Taylor first contacted me for a coaching session, she said she thought she needed just a little help staying focused. She sent her business website address along with her inquiry email. She was a photographer, and the photo on her "About" page showed a woman with warm brown eyes and a wide smile. She had recently gone through some major transitions. Within a year, she had married, bought a new home, and changed careers from banking to being a self-employed freelance wedding photographer.

Change was everywhere in Taylor's life, and she was struggling with how intense it all felt. As it turned out, help with staying focused was only part of what was going on. We began our work together and started to hone in on what Taylor really wanted, and she immediately started using the tool of accessing the body. After a few coaching sessions, Taylor had done some self-investigation into her predominant fear routine.

"Pessimist," she said, reporting back after having done some Courage Habit exercises between our calls. "I hate admitting that, but that's what I see. Every single time something doesn't go smoothly, I just want to give up. I feel like it's impossible. If we find some new repair that didn't turn up on the inspection report when we bought the house, I immediately want to throw in the towel and say that we never should have bought the house. Or, if someone I talked to about getting portraits done ends up not calling back, I just want to check out and watch television."

When Taylor went into a Pessimist headspace, she felt sure that nothing could be counted upon to work out, and since nothing was going to work out anyway, she might as well do something else. Of course, this mind-set only made things harder, and every time she "checked out" with the temporary reward of a *Grey's Anatomy* binge, she'd feel better for a few hours, but later she would feel stressed and disappointed in herself because she hadn't worked on her business.

Taylor had taken a big risk stepping away from salaried employment and into a career that she was truly excited about. (This risk I could relate to!) If she wanted to feel resilient in the face of change or make progress toward her dream of being a professional photographer, Taylor would have to become aware of the times she goes into Pessimist routines, because they were undermining her at every turn.

To do that, our work started with the first step of the Courage Habit. In stopping to access her body, Taylor began to recognize the sensations of fear that acted like cues, such as a fearful brain-fog that caused her to feel anxious and trip over her words when she was on the phone with a potential client. Accessing the body as a regular practice helped her to recognize what was happening in the moment. It also helped her feel more grounded during client calls.

Taylor was making great strides in the right direction, but she still struggled after setbacks. She noticed something that she hadn't paid as much attention to before: a persistent, critical inner voice that was always there to tell Taylor that she didn't have what it took to run a business. "Of course that client didn't hire you. What made you think you could run a business, anyway? You're a hobby photographer, not a professional." No matter how many times Taylor tapped into her body to try to make that inner critical voice go away, it just wouldn't stay silent.

Taylor isn't the only one who gets stuck when that inner voice of criticism or pessimism pipes up. We all have these critical inner voices, and I'm not talking about schizophrenia or a psychological disorder. These critical voices are the internalized voices of criticism—blame, judgment, condescension, defeat, put-downs, and downplaying or abandoning progress. In other words, it's how we talk to ourselves when we don't feel capable or when we're feeling "less than." These voices often parallel those of the people who raised us, a dominant group that projects stereotypes onto the gender or culture that we are part of, or our fear routines. (Perfectionist critical voices, for instance, will push for more perfection, while Pessimist critical voices will say that there's no point in trying). I call these collective internalized voices the "Inner Critic" or just the "Critic," because it's a neutral term that objectively labels what these voices are doing.

Think you don't have a Critic? I'd urge you to reconsider that. All too often, the denial of the Critic's existence means that the Critic is exerting even *more* power over someone's life. In her research into people's experiences of shame, Dr. Brenè Brown found that the more someone denied feeling any shame, the more shame was at work in his or her life. Working directly with hundreds of clients, retreat participants, and workshop trainees for more than a decade, I've found the same to be true with the denial of the Critic. Absolutely everyone has one, even the most confident people you know. The more that people insist that they have no critical voices or that they're "in control" of those voices, the more those voices run them in circles, and they don't even realize it.

In the last chapter, you learned about the first step of the Courage Habit: accessing the body. You now know how to recognize fear sensations that might cue a fear routine. With body-based practices that you can use when you notice fear or self-doubt taking over, you can slow down enough to take the next step in the Courage Habit: listening without attachment. In this chapter, you'll learn about more effective approaches to work with those Inner Critic voices, rather than avoiding or fighting against them. You'll start to relate to your Inner Critic in a new way that diffuses its ability to intimidate you right when you're going after a big dream and bringing your most courageous self to light.

Many people start out like Taylor did, detached from their Inner Critic voices, relegating them to the background noise of their lives until they don't even notice them anymore. It was when Taylor started to tune in to her body that she became aware of this voice, and that's when she realized she needed a new way of responding to this voice, rather than ignoring it or telling it to go away. Wanting to avoid your Critic or tell it to go away is understandable, because tuning in to what the Critic says is challenging and stressful. Karen Horney, a pioneering feminist psychologist, theorized that people respond to relationship stress by trying to get their needs met in one of three ways: detachment, compliance, or aggression.

We try to survive our interactions with the Inner Critic in the same ways. I call it *avoiding, pleasing,* and *attacking.* When people are *avoiding* dealing with their Critic, as Saboteurs or Pessimists do, they're trying to tune out the Critic's words. They might do this through procrastination (putting off or rationalizing waiting to take action), distraction (through overwork, turning to alcohol or other chemicals), or resistance to following through (such as not using tools that could help them, like practicing the Courage Habit regularly).

Pleasing the Critic, which is common for Perfectionists and Martyrs, translates as trying harder to "do it right," whatever "it" is, so that the Critic won't have anything to say. For example, if a Perfectionist's Critic says that she needs to be better, she responds by doubling down her efforts, with the logic that if she is better, the Critic will be satisfied. The problem? The Critic is never satisfied. Martyrs who want to keep the peace and be noticed for their efforts, follow the same path of trying to please the Critic so that it will leave them alone, yet they meet the same result.

Attacking the Critic is arguing with it or responding to its voice aggressively. It's fighting back with words, such as "What do you know, anyway?" or "Shut up," or "Fuck off." Pinterest graphics with messages, such as "Today's the day I kick fear's ass" fall into this category. Just about everyone, when they feel like they've hit their limit with the internal abuse, will have at least some moment where they try attacking the Critic. While fighting back can give you a rush of feeling more powerful or in control, this too is ultimately exhausting and futile. After all, telling your Critic to go away has not made it go away forever, has it? Instead of doing the things we've done before that are only temporarily helpful, we need to find new ways of relating to the Critic that go beyond attacking back and being locked in a battle.

Let's begin the process by considering how you've been responding to your Critic. What do you find yourself doing most often? Do you tend to avoid, please, or push? Can you find any concrete evidence that avoiding, pleasing, or attacking is a sustainable or effective strategy for the rest of your life? Use the Courage Habit step of accessing the body to really pause, breathe, and honestly answer these questions.

If the idea of being in conflict with this Critic voice for the rest of your life sounds exhausting or unappealing, then there's some good news. Learning to listen without attachment to the Critic will be the game changer. When you're feeling pulled into the fears of the Critic, slowing down to listen without attachment prepares you to tune in and really listen to what your Critic is saying. You're directly facing that fearful voice within.

"Listening without attachment is very conscious," I told Taylor the day that we talked about adding this second step to her practice of accessing the body. "You're listening to the Critic's actual words, which is—no lie—uncomfortable. But, you're not *just* listening. You're listening *without attachment*. You're consciously deciding not to get attached to what the Critic says. I compare it to if you encountered a drunk person on the street who was insisting that you're a bad person. You might *hear* the words the person was saying, but you'd ultimately decide not to *lend any authority* to his words."

Taylor had spent a long time tuning out her Critic, and it had never worked. To shift her old fear patterns, she needed to stop avoiding, pleasing, or attacking her Critic and start listening, but doing so intentionally without giving power to the Critic.

Investigating the Critic

To investigate the Critic, we've got to do what most of us, like Taylor, avoid for as long as possible: listen to what the Critic has to say. That's how we lay the groundwork for seeing how critical voices operate. For the exercise that follows, I strongly encourage you to write down your answers. (You can also download a worksheet for this "Investigating the Critic" exercise at the website for this book at http://www.yourcourageouslife.com/courage-habit.) When I work with a coaching client, we complete this exercise together. You could answer these questions on your own or with a partner, coach, therapist, or friend.

As you write down your answers, it's important that you capture exactly what the Critic *says* and how it sounds. For instance, instead of writing "I'm afraid of failing," write what your Critic *says* to you when you fear failure, the way that the voice sounds in your head: "Who do you think you are?" "You'll never finish this." "Someone else has already done it, better." Capturing the Critic's exact words is important for how we will pull apart its influence in later exercises.

1. How does your Critic show up? What are the things it most commonly says to you? This could include reasons for why change is too hard or you aren't capable, judgments of your character ("lazy," "stupid"), catastrophizing ("If I fail, it will be impossible to recover"), or bringing up mistakes you've made. Set a timer for five minutes and really try to write absolutely everything you can think of. Think of this step as getting everything out in the open.

2. Next, get honest about your own relationship with the Critic. How do you tend to regard your Inner Critic? How do you feel about the fact that there are these aspects of you? For example, do you resent that it's there, despite your best efforts? Are you exhausted by it? Are you tired of it? What's your truth?

3. Consider the Primary Focus that you articulated in Chapter 1, and the life that your most courageous self would be living. You probably hit on some big dreams or desires for change, such as working on a difficult relationship, having more fun in life, or doing something specific like traveling the world. When the Critic weighs in on your ability to make those changes or achieve that dream, what does it say to you about your limitations or incapability? Go beyond "not enough money" or "not enough time."

After you write down everything that you can think of, there's an important final piece to complete the exercise. Revisit the first part of the Courage Habit process, accessing the body, using whichever approach you found most helpful. (In other words, take some time to dance, cry, breathe slowly, take a walk, or otherwise tune in to your body.) Without exception, everyone who really goes into this exercise with their whole heart will find it challenging to listen to their fearful inner voices. Take care of yourself so that you can get to the other side of any fears that have limited your life, rather than getting stuck in this part of the process. Accessing the body becomes a tool to lean on so that you don't unconsciously go into a fear routine.

The reason so many of us avoid dealing with our Critic is now written down on a piece of paper in front of you. The voice of the Critic is messy, often mean, and it can be extremely difficult to face those thoughts and feelings at once. Remember, these are *just words on paper*. These words don't have to "mean" anything about you or your life. By writing down the Critic's words, and then deciding to access the body rather than avoid, please, or attack, you're already starting to reroute the cue-routine-reward process that would have pulled you back into old, fear-based habits. It's this practice of listening intently, but without giving authority to the Critic or doing what it says, that's so important to shifting the power the Critic has. Now, you stand poised to untangle yourself from getting stuck.

Untangling the Critic's Voice

As Taylor began listening to and writing down exactly what her Critic said, she began to see why it had been so tempting to try to ignore it entirely. She noticed that her Critic wasn't only showing up as belittling or sarcastic. Sometimes her Critic would shape-shift, always expecting more of her or suddenly turning the tables when she least expected it. Taylor's Critic could work both sides of an argument like a master. If she worked hard to market her photography business, the Critic insisted that she should have worked *harder*. Other times, when she did work harder and really put herself out there, she found herself stressed out, overwhelmed, and getting sick. That's when the Critic would twist its message and say that Taylor worked *too* much, her life was out of balance, and that her sickness was evidence that she'd never make self-employment sustainable.

Taylor also noticed that her Critic could be downright vicious. As she tuned in more, she truly struggled because she felt nervous on client calls and didn't quite know what to do when she heard the Critic say, in a tone of condescension and disgust, "How is a client ever going to hire you if you sound like a nervous idiot on the phone?" Even more confusing were the times when the Critic used logical reasoning to undermine her, such as when Taylor connected with other professional photographers and her Critic casually and calmly pointed out, "Their websites are better and they're always going to get more clients. Let's be honest: you aren't even in their league. Don't go getting your hopes up."

When we are untangling from the power that our Critic voices hold over us, we all do this dance with competing voices, and things get confusing. What *is* the difference between a logical-yet-malicious Critic and our own common sense about right and wrong? After all, Taylor wondered, wasn't it *true* that clients wouldn't hire her if she "sounded like an idiot" on the phone? Wasn't it true that a better website would be more likely to result in getting more clients? If her Critic wasn't being loud and aggressive in pointing this out to her, wouldn't she just get complacent? Would she be motivated to change without this voice?

I could relate to this confusion, because when I'd first started to unhook from my own Perfectionist routine, it had been difficult for me to tell the difference between my own internal standards of excellence versus the striving standards of my Critic. How could I know the difference between pushing myself in a way that was healthy, versus striving for endless perfection?

To distinguish the difference between yourself and your Critic, there are two things to notice. First, notice how the voice of the Critic mirrors your fear routines. For example, the Critic showing up as a Perfectionist is solely focused on the result yet is never truly satisfied, whereas healthy striving for a goal involves taking time to reflect and appreciate hard work throughout the process. The Martyr sees the pleased look on people's faces and takes that as validation that sacrificing her own ambitions (yet again) was worth it, whereas someone practicing interdependence will give as generously to herself as she does to others. The Pessimist really does think she sees all the evidence for why nothing will work out after one small disappointment, and the person who puts disappointment in its proper context feels what's real without turning feelings into evidence that nothing else is possible. The Saboteur buries her head in the sand when she's not following through on a commitment yet again, but someone who's self-aware will notice that constantly moving on to the next thing isn't in her long-term best interest.

The second thing you can notice is where you end up when you ask yourself "Is this helpful?" Is the internal voice offering information or insight that's truly helpful? How do you *feel* when you hear this internal voice? Do you feel energized when you think about what this voice is saying? Does the voice offer you information that helps you to work through what you're facing? If not, it's probably the voice of the Critic.

Sometimes people tell me that they can't tell the difference between what's really their Critic versus who they truly are. They've been listening to the Critic voices for so long that they feel cut off from their intuition and authentic self, which makes untangling the voices so intimidating and frustrating that they want to throw up their hands. This is an extremely common response to this work, and I'd invite you to dig deep and trust the process, even if all the untangling doesn't happen after one exercise. When it's extremely difficult to tell the difference between the Critic and the "real you," this means that a process called "fusion" has taken place. *Fusion*, which comes from acceptance and commitment therapy (ACT), is what has happened when we believe that what we think is synonymous with who we are, and we behave accordingly. As therapist Steven Hayes puts it, "Fusion means getting caught up in our thoughts and allowing them to dominate our behavior" (2009). In those moments when your Critic tells you that something isn't possible or can't or shouldn't be done, and you believe the voice and act on it, you're "fused" with the Critic.

Nearly all of us are fused with our Critics, until we stop to ask ourselves what the Critic is saying. As you get more practice with the Courage Habit step of listening without attachment, it gets easier to recognize the difference between the "real you" and the Critic's punishing standards. As I would remind any client, be gentle with yourself when it seems "too big" to parse, and remember that your old habits took time to create, and they will take time to undo. Keep integrating the Courage Habit step of accessing the body, and every time you get stuck make sure that you pause to cry the tears, punch the air in frustration, dance vigorously to get the blood flowing, or slow down and breathe.

Taylor's question about how to tell the difference between herself and the Critic was answered as soon as I asked her about her fear routine. "Usually, when we take a healthy break from something, we feel rejuvenated in some way. When you go into the fear routine of the Pessimist and stop working toward your goals, does that nourish you?" I asked.

"Nourish me? No, I wouldn't call it that. It's more of that checking out feeling," Taylor said. For Taylor to tell the difference between who she really was versus what her Critic was saying, Taylor turned to what she had already uncovered about her Pessimist fear routine, which was all about giving up when things got tough. Giving up never gave her the sort of rejuvenating break that left her feeling rested and ready to be even more of her most courageous self. I also encouraged Taylor to access the body when she took breaks to see what she felt internally. Taylor found that when she took breaks from work because she was in her Pessimist routine, she'd feel a sensation of just wanting to "check out," and taking a break under those conditions never refueled her.

Consider which fear routine you identified with in Chapter 2: Martyr, Pessimist, Perfectionist, or Saboteur. The description of each routine included some examples of what you're likely to say to yourself when you're in the middle of that fear routine. Those examples are in fact examples of the voices of the Critic. Do you see the connection between what your Critic says to you, and how that perpetuates that fear routine? Pause and take time to write in a journal or on a piece of paper anything that seems particularly significant.

Your Best Friend (with Lousy Communication Skills)

I've been talking about the fact that the Critic exists and you've been exploring how yours shows up, but we haven't yet looked at the questions that dogged me for the longest time. *Why* is the Critic so caught in a fear routine? Why isn't stopping the Critic just as simple as telling it to go away, or refusing to pay attention to it? Logically it seems like it should be that simple, but in practice it never is.

The answers to these questions start with revisiting what we know about the basal ganglia and cue-routine-reward. Remember that with the cue-routine-reward, we feel the cue of fear, and the basal ganglia prompts us to move into whichever routine gets us to the fastest "reward" of reduced tension. When Taylor's Critic berated her, its voice was dysfunctional and stress inducing. But, for Taylor, the Critic's voice was never as stress inducing as *actually taking action* toward her big dream. That big dream was new, uncertain, and therefore a bigger deal because it was emotionally riskier. Every time Taylor backed down and checked out, she got her temporary "reward" of reduced tension. To stop getting stuck in the same cycle, she needed to keep coming back to the essential work of slowing down to access the body, remember that her Pessimist fear routine might be at work, and make a conscious choice to listen in to what the Critic was saying. Consistently practicing each piece of the Courage Habit in tandem was essential.

Your fear routine might be different than Taylor's, but it will play out the same way. For example, when I felt fear, I went into my Perfectionist fear routine, which drove me to overwork. While it was stressful when my perfectionist Critic would berate me, it was still more familiar to do what the Critic said, because *that's what I was used to doing.* Our fear routines are habituated and will always feel, at the beginning, more comfortable to turn to than trying something entirely new.

The Big Secret About the Critic

Here's the big "secret" about the Critic: The Critic is invested in a fear routine, and it won't go away just because we want it to. It thinks that by criticizing you it's protecting you.

Underneath the condescension, shape-shifting, malicious logic, yelling, berating, and intimidation, the Critic is, in fact, *scared*. It's scared of change and it's scared of doing things differently. It's scared of living differently, experiencing rejection, and dealing with failure. The Critic is not out to get you. It's wounded and it's trying to protect you from future wounding. It's from that wounded place of fear that the Critic starts to criticize you, hoping that if you stay in the old, familiar routines, you'll be safe from any harm.

I still remember how I felt the day that my coach, Matthew Marzel, suggested his own alternative interpretation of the Critic: "It's your best friend with lousy communication skills," he said. Immediately, I felt revulsion: *No way* was this Critic "my friend!" This voice that constantly undermined me right when I was trying to do something new? This voice that was always pointing out what could go wrong? Was he kidding?

"I see the Critic as being the part of us that is interested in survival at all costs," Matthew explained. "For as loud as it can be, it's actually incredibly insecure and afraid. It sees going after your dreams as a terrible threat, one that could come with rejection and feelings of failure. So, the Critic is going to do whatever it takes to avoid those experiences, even if that means speaking to you in ways that are abusive to stop you from taking a risk. It's trying to keep you safe, but it has lousy communication skills. I've made a commitment to set boundaries with my Critic, rather than ignore it or attack back."

Then, Matthew wanted to know: Had ignoring, placating, or fighting the Critic ever succeeded at making it go away? When I examined that question, I realized that no, it hadn't. My Critic always came back, so the work of avoiding, pleasing, or attacking was endless (and exhausting). For the first time, with Matthew's help, I began to listen to the specific things the Critic was telling me and tried to see the fear that was behind the Critic's words.

For instance, the Critic had often said that my writing was shit and that I'd never get published. That voice was the fear of failure. When the Critic said this I avoided writing to not think about the possibility of failure. Or, I pushed myself relentlessly, buying into the illusion that an exhausting effort would guarantee the results I wanted. *No pain, no gain, right?* The Critic also told me that I was selfish and didn't do enough for others. This represented my fear of not being likable enough unless I overcompensated and proved myself through doing acts of service. The Critic used judgment and condescension to make me afraid of not being liked, and in turn to push me to work harder by piling on the good deeds for other people. While wanting to be liked isn't a bad thing, being driven by the Critic's fear of rejection was an exhausting way to live. The Critic's fear was in the driver's seat, not my own desires to live from the value of courage.

After so many years of listening to my own Critic, and the Critics of so many clients and workshop attendees, talk a big game while being afraid and insecure at the core, I could see the same thing playing out in Taylor's life. Her Critic was always looking out for her from a place of wanting to protect her from being rejected, and it used terrible communication as a misguided attempt at protection. If the Critic could berate her into not taking action, then maybe she wouldn't take a risk that could involve failure—real or imagined. The Critic was trying, in its own dysfunctional way, to stop her from encountering pain.

Try this out for yourself. Revisit your answers to the "Investigating the Critic" exercise and look at the specific things that you wrote down, this time with an eye for seeing where the Critic is using bullying, intimidation, criticism, shaming, or something else to keep you from taking action toward your goals. What could its true agenda be in keeping you from taking risks? Does your Critic tell you that you're not good enough? That other people will think your ideas are stupid? That so-and-so has already done what you want to do, and better, so there's no point? Then ask yourself *why* the Critic might say those things, and how saying those things is your Critic behaving as your "best friend with lousy communication skills."

If you believe what the Critic says and you back down from what you really want, then you never invite the risks that come with taking a chance on your biggest dreams. For your Critic, that short-term safety is worth it. Now you get to decide if it's worth it to keep believing what the Critic tells you or if it's time to change.

Change starts with having a different relationship with the Critic. It's neither your enemy nor the person who should be giving you advice. Rather, it's an insecure, fear-based aspect of ourselves that has one agenda: *staying safe.*

"To help myself not go into avoiding, pleasing, or attack, I try to think of my Critic as being like a small child," I told Taylor. "It's got limited skills for handling stress, and it tends to go for short-term thinking and immediate gratification. If I was encountering a small child throwing a temper tantrum, would it be effective to lock that child in a room to avoid him? If I please the child and give him whatever he wants, that might stop the tantrum, but there would always be more demands. The worst option, of course, is attack. If I attack a small child when he is throwing a tantrum, I end up doing more damage if he is screaming at me and I scream back. I become the abuser."

"This makes me think of when my husband and I are in an argument," Taylor said. "If we slam doors and avoid each other, it doesn't help. If I say that I'm sorry when I'm really not feeling that way just to try to end the fight, that doesn't help. And, I hate it when he does that with me. The worst is when I say something to him that I'll regret."

I was so glad that Taylor was making the connection between relating to her Critic and relating to other people in her life, especially because the notion of "kicking fear's ass" is so rampant in our culture's discussions of how to handle fear. Instead of seeing the Critic as something to be done away with, she was opening up to the idea that she could have the same investment in working things out with her Critic as she does with her husband.

What I knew from personal experience was that something even better was possible: The Critic's angry, frightened behavior, when responded to with a mixture of compassion and boundaries, could *heal*. It's the mixture of the two—compassion and boundaries—that is so radically transformative when working with the Critic.

Cracking the Critic's Code

The idea of seeing her Critic as a small child with limited skills had been helpful to Taylor in not going into avoidance, pleasing, or attack modes. She was stopping the habitual cycle of her fear routine.

"I feel like I'm starting to get all these different pieces and pulling them together," Taylor told me. "I'm noticing what I need more, especially when the Pessimist routine is coming up, because I'm accessing the body. I'm hearing what my Critic has to say, which is still weird, but okay. I'm game. But, I keep wondering: If my Critic really is so afraid…what is the Critic so afraid *of*? I mean, I was never abused when I was growing up. I can't think of any big trauma that I've survived. To be honest, I feel kind of bad when I consider the things that other people have gone through, and how charmed my life has been by comparison. I'm really lucky, and I have so much to be thankful for, so why am I so stuck like this?"

It was a question that I had contemplated many times myself, and I'd had more than one conversation that bordered on existential angst with friends about this. As humans are we just inherently fragile? Was this just the human condition? Was this the result of collective communities giving way to isolated societies? Was it something biochemical? Why was there this aspect of the self that seemed so fundamentally insecure? There was only one answer that seemed appropriate: the Critic was fundamentally afraid because life is fundamentally uncertain, and we live in a world that we can't control.

So, that's what I told her. "I think that the Critic clings to this illusion or idea that somehow you should be able to control your life better. You could control it through working harder, or you could control it through never making mistakes. You could control it by making endless plans. You could control it through being thinner, prettier, smarter, or richer."

"It's the shape-shifting!" Taylor said, as she put the pieces together. "*Control* is what's behind the Critic's shape-shifting. If I work more, I should have worked harder, and if I work so hard that I get sick, I should have known better to stop and take a break. It's this thing where I'm always supposed to be in control somehow."

"You've got it," I said. "And, really, what's happening is something that the Critic doesn't want to face: Life itself is imperfect and bad things happen to good people. No one's life ever looks as good as their Pinterest boards. No one ever achieves the lives they dream of without struggle. No one is in control! The Critic is terrified of this lack of control, so it's striving and clinging for safety. In the name of safety, the Critic will do whatever it takes. It'll tell you that there's no point in trying and then berate you for not having tried harder. It's illogical because it's terrified."

The idea made sense to Taylor, but it also brought up another unappealing possibility: Did this mean that she'd always need to put up with hearing the Critic's anger and condescension, and there was nothing more to be done about it? I reminded her that listening without attachment meant listening without lending *authority* to the Critic's voice. I told her that she could hear the words without necessarily believing them or doing what the Critic said. "But there is one other piece that's helpful," I added. "Once you know what the Critic says, it's time for implementing some boundaries."

Boundaries, with the Critic? At first, this idea usually feels impossible. Clients are often skeptical when I tell them that there *is* a process they can use to help transform even the angriest, meanest, most judgmental critical voices. Since this work is never about becoming "fearless" and since we know that avoiding, pleasing, and attacking don't work, the strategies that I'll share aren't about different ways to ignore the voices or telling them to go away. Instead, we start changing your *relationship* to your Critic. After learning to listen to its voice without getting hooked by what it says, you throw down some very real, no-nonsense boundaries.

"Re-Do, Please"

We've arrived at the most effective tool for working with Critic voices that I've ever come across. This is a tool that my coach Matthew originally taught me, and I've now passed it on to hundreds of people in one-on-one coaching sessions, workshops, and large-scale telesummits and online classes. It's called, "Re-do, Please."

I've found that it's easiest to understand how you use "Re-do, Please" with your Critic if you first imagine how you'd use it with another person. My husband and I have certainly had practice with this tool! Between two people, "Re-do, Please" would work like this: whenever either you or your partner says something that feels tense, disrespectful, or unloving to the other, you commit to asking for a "Re-do, Please."

For example, let's say that my husband forgets something at the store that I needed for dinner. He gets home and I'm frustrated. Without thinking, I say, "Seriously? You forgot that, again? I'm so sick of you forgetting to swing by the store when I ask you to."

Then, my husband says (usually after taking a breath and accessing the body): "Uh, re-do, please." That's his signal to me that I've said something that isn't feeling respectful, and he'd like me to rephrase it.

After taking a breath, accessing the body, and noticing what I'm feeling, I say, "Okay, okay. I'm sorry. I'm feeling overwhelmed and upset because we're out of this ingredient. I really need it for dinner tonight. Can you go to the store?"

The tone of "Re-do, Please" is the most important part of its efficacy as a tool. The delivery is matter-of-fact, rather than passive-aggressively conveying through tone that deep down you're still pissed. You would practice the tool of "Re-do, Please" in the same way with your Critic. When it says something negative to you, you can kindly say to the Critic, "Re-do, please. I'm open to hearing what you have to say, but it needs to be phrased respectfully."

When Taylor first began practicing this with the things her Critic said, it sounded something like this:

Critic: How is a client ever going to hire you if you sound like an idiot?

Taylor: (After taking a breath and accessing the body) Re-do, please. I'm open to hearing what you're saying, but I need you to respectfully rephrase that.

Taylor's Critic didn't automatically become chipper and positive when she asked the Critic to communicate respectfully. It said things like: "That's bullshit. I'm not a liar. No client will hire you if you sound like an idiot, and that's just the truth." If the Critic's tone or words were not respectful, Taylor would respond with: "Re-do, please. I'm open to hearing this, but it must be respectful. Re-do, please."

Taylor's Critic didn't give up right away. It responded with softening its words, but still sounding unsupportive: "Whatever.

It's just not a smart move to quit your day job when you're that nervous on the phone. That's a basic part of this whole freelance thing, and you can't handle it." Whenever Taylor's Critic shifted slightly but remained critical, Taylor would speak to that: "I see how you shifted the words, yet this still isn't supportive. I need us to speak to each other in a way that is supportive and respectful. Perhaps you might tell me what you're most afraid of? Re-do, please."

It was at that point that Taylor's Critic arrived at the real fear: "I'm terrified that if you fail at this business, you won't have money to pay the bills. I'm terrified that your husband will resent you for sinking your money into this. I'm terrified that if we fail at this, it'll mean that you'll work at a job you hate for the rest of your life, and that's just that."

As soon as your Critic, like Taylor's, starts to communicate what it is afraid of and drops the judgment that was covering over that fear, you and your Critic are ready to work with what's at the core. When the Critic drops its defensiveness, you're speaking with the wound in need of healing, rather than the armor that keeps the old routine in place.

"What are you really, truly afraid of?" That's the question that you want to ask your Critic once the defensiveness has dropped. If the Critic will tell you what it's afraid of, then you can start to build resilience in that area. When Taylor's Critic was spinning in its own fears about money, being resented by her husband, or failing at doing what she loved, it was only churning the fears over and over again. That kept her feeling stuck. Through dialoguing with the Critic and using "Re-do, Please," Taylor could hear what her Critic was afraid of, and regard her Critic with tenderness and care, rather than attacking, pleasing, or avoiding.

She could see how her wounded Critic was like a small child in need of healing, rather than an enemy that she needed to conquer.

Using "Re-Do, Please"

Try the "Re-do, Please" process for yourself. Start by revisiting your answers to the "Investigating the Critic" exercise from earlier in this chapter. Take each statement from that exercise one at a time, and try saying it out loud and listen for what your Critic says. Each time the Critic says something that doesn't feel respectful or supportive, respond with the statement "Re-do, please" to gently share with your Critic what you need. For example, if the Critic's tone is harsh, say, "Re-do, please. I want to hear what you're trying to say, but I need to hear a kinder, more neutral tone." Repeat "Re-do, Please" with every harsh response your Critic comes up with until you get down to the fear that's at the core of that Critic statement. (This exercise is also available as a worksheet and guided meditation, at http://www.yourcourageouslife.com /courage-habit.) You can also have a powerful experience with this exercise if you record it or speak out loud while looking into a mirror.

The process will follow a back-and-forth, in which you write down what the Critic says, and then keep responding to what it says with "Re-do, please. I want to hear what you have to say, and I'm committed to respectful communication. Please rephrase that. Re-do, please."

As you continue to respond, you're looking for the moment when the Critic is willing to get real about what it fears and step into some vulnerability. Until then, every time the Critic offers some statement that isn't supportive either in words or tone, say "Re-do, please," and add something that establishes boundaries with the Critic. Give it kind directions for exactly what needs to change in order for it to hopefully rephrase its message. If the Critic uses calm, reasonable logic but with an undertone that isn't supportive, ask the Critic to rephrase using a statement that is supportive.

This exercise is a powerful practice for creating respectful communication from your Critic. You are drawing a boundary line: The Critic will be listened to, you will no longer go into attack mode, and the Critic cannot attack either. You won't allow it to be disrespectful.

Expect this process to be one that you repeat regularly and return to any time things are challenging. You don't "get rid of" your Critic. You just keep uncovering more and more layers of what it is afraid of and processing those layers. Through processing each of the Critic's fears, you find freedom *from* the fear.

Meeting the Critic's Needs

"Let's go back to that image of a small child," I suggested to Taylor when we arrived at her Critic's deepest fears—not having enough money, being resented, or working a job she disliked for the rest of her life. "If you were sitting next to a small child, and she said she was afraid of not having enough money, what would you do?"

Taylor started to get emotional as she took a breath and shared what came next. I could imagine her brown eyes filling with tears, as she told me about just how tight money had been for her family when she was a kid. Her parents had both hated their jobs, and it wore on them and caused them to take out their frustration in the form of fighting with each other in front of Taylor, or being irritable and impatient with Taylor any time she needed lunch money for school or new school supplies. When Taylor was ten years old, a big rift occurred. Taylor's father had loaned money to Taylor's uncle without telling Taylor's mother first. Her uncle never paid the money back and her mother never forgave her father.

"That sounds like it was enormously difficult to watch, especially as a child," I said. We were both quiet for a moment. Then I asked, "If you were with that ten-year-old you right now, what kind of support would you give her? Even if you couldn't control life and make money appear or stop the fighting, but you were there to support that ten-year-old you, what would you do?"

"I'd let her know that we turned out okay," Taylor said, without hesitation. "Even without the money, we turned out okay."

That session with Taylor was an incredibly intense, emotional session in which I myself felt tears coming to my eyes as she made connections between her present-day circumstances and the Critic that was trying desperately not to experience financial hardships or someone else's resentment. It was one of those sessions where tough memories were recounted, but a powerful thread was emerging. Taylor confirmed for me that even though there had been a lack of money and plenty of fear growing up, nothing she deeply feared had truly come to fruition.

The Critic that screamed or nagged in her head in its search for safety had distracted Taylor from the most important facts of her life's story. She had developed resilience through hardship, and that resilience mattered more than the fact that she'd endured hardship. Even though she was imperfect and had found herself going into Pessimist mode on more than one occasion, she had been committed enough to her dreams and living from the place of her most courageous self to decide to seek help working with fear and self-doubt as it arose.

One last time, I'd like to ask that you turn back to the "Investigating the Critic" exercise, and review what it is that your Critic says to you. At this point, you might notice that some of what the Critic says fails to have as much impact because you've read the words so many times that you now see where it's just afraid and says things that are untrue.

However, this time look for the things that the Critic says that you know would still hook you. Examine anything that the Critic might say that would be difficult to be with and try to clearly understand the Critic's agenda, or its reason for trying to keep you from taking a step forward. Pay attention to how the Critic's reasoning is rooted in a dysfunctional need for safety. Use the tool of "Re-do, Please" with those statements until you get to the bottom of what the Critic is afraid of. Or, try asking the Critic: "What are you really afraid of? What's really going on here?"

In the weeks that followed, there was a powerful fierceness that was starting to arise in Taylor and show up in every area of her life. Taylor's Primary Focus had been to grow her photography business to support her, and now she was applying the Courage Habit step of listening without attachment any time the Critic showed up around that goal.

During our calls, she was fully claiming the fact that she had legitimate desires for her life, and what's more, she was worthy of them. Even when she had days where she felt resistant, she was keeping more perspective than before. Accessing the body had given her the ability to feel resistance or frustration, and then process it by taking walks or stopping to breathe. Listening to the Critic without getting hooked by what it said, and using tools like "Re-do, Please" to set boundaries and get to the root of the Critic's fear had put Taylor in charge of her life.

The quality of our sessions had changed, and now we were moving at a fast clip. Instead of hearing about all the reasons why something "would never work," now I was hearing about all the options that might be possible. She also started to see more regular requests for portrait sessions coming through, and she and her husband had sat down to map out a financial plan for themselves without fighting.

"Admittedly, a glass of wine while we ran the numbers probably helped," Taylor said, laughing. I was so happy to hear the lightness in her voice, and I knew that she was proud of herself, too. Taylor had learned the most fundamental lesson in allowing her most courageous self to come forward: The Critic is part of who we are, a piece of the whole. If you want to love and accept who you are fully, then that will include learning how to love and accept the pieces that are messier or harder to be with, such as the Critic. We often fear that if we give the Critic our attention, it will just grow bigger and louder. Instead, Taylor found that the power of love and compassion for healing the Critic's wounding was the real key to her freedom.

Moving Forward

This chapter has covered a lot of essential ground. I'm always encouraging clients to remember to keep leaning on that first tool of accessing the body, in whatever way they can, so that they can stay present to the process that they're in. I encourage the same for you. What body-based practice can you do for even five minutes after reading this chapter?

It's also important that as we work through each part of the Courage Habit, you keep circling back to your Primary Focus. Remind yourself of what your Primary Focus goals are, and be very clear about the exact words your Critic uses to convince you that those dreams either aren't worth pursuing, or that you aren't capable of creating the life that you want. After Taylor uncovered some of her Critic's deepest fears, she had more awareness of what her Critic was most likely to say when she was taking steps toward her Primary Focus. She returned to using the "Re-do, Please" tool every time the Critic showed up. Having a specific check-in around just her Primary Focus goals helped her to feel more focused with the changes that she was making.

We're now halfway through the four parts of the Courage Habit. All the pieces work in tandem, but once you know how to access the body and listen without attachment, you're ready for step three: *reframing limiting Stories.* By the time a fear pattern is in place, we've all spent far too long believing in limited, narrow views of what's possible for our lives. Reframing limiting Stories is where we go once we know what the Critic is saying and we're ready to give it a new Story to follow.

Chapter 5

Reframing Limiting Stories

For years, I'd been doing the strangest thing. I would get up early, sometimes as early as five or six in the morning, to drive to half marathons or triathlons where I was only ever a spectator. Athletes fascinated me, particularly those who took on long distances. How did they do that? How did they put their bodies through such taxing circumstances? I was fascinated by what they could do, but I believed that there was no way that I could do that. Instead, I read books about endurance sports and subscribed to magazines like *Triathlete* and *Runner's World*.

I only watched from afar and read books about endurance racing because, in my estimation, I was too physically weak to race. After all, I reminded myself, it wasn't like I was an "athlete," and I certainly wasn't a triathlete who could swim, bike, and run. I was, at best, a "can keep myself afloat" swimmer, an easily tired cyclist, and while I liked running, I seemed to have a penchant for injuries.

But, secretly I *wanted* to be a triathlete. No, I *yearned* to be a triathlete. When I watched Ironman replays on YouTube, my heart would quicken. That's why I kept reading about racing, showing up at races, and buying actual DVD documentaries about endurance events. In the back of my mind, every time I saw something about mega-endurance triathlon training, a small inner voice would whisper, "Ooooooh! I want to do that!" But, for years, just as quickly as that voice came up, I'd sigh and think, "Would be nice, but I couldn't do it. I'm not an athlete."

This thought wasn't the harsh, condescending voice of the Critic. If it had been, I'd have paid more attention to it. Instead, this thought was simple, matter-of-fact: *The sky was blue, the grass was green, and Kate was not an athlete.* Nevertheless, one day I got it in my head that I wanted to go to a sporting-goods store and try on a triathlon wet suit just to see what it was like. I had no idea that putting on a wet suit was an aerobic endeavor unto itself until I was grunting and sweating to pull the neoprene over my hips in a changing room. I was shaped more like Kate Winslet than like the narrow, muscular bodies of the women I saw in *Triathlete* magazine. I looked at myself in the mirror, the wet suit only halfway on, while the salesperson outside asked if I needed anything because I'd been in the changing room for so long. I thought to myself, "Kate, what are you doing trying to pull this thing on? You're not an athlete."

But then, that inner voice, the voice that I think of as my most courageous self, quietly mentioned: "Even if you aren't an athlete right now, maybe you could become one." This idea, while obvious when printed here in black and white, felt strange to consider. Then my most courageous self continued to speak to me: "Even if you feel ridiculous putting on a wet suit right now, by the time you do a few triathlons, putting on a wet suit would just be normal. Anything that you do often enough, after all, becomes a 'normal' kind of thing."

In that moment, I started to see the limiting "capital-S Story" that had been undermining me for so long. This Story had not been the voice of the Critic tearing me down. Rather, it had been a simple assumption: *I was not an athlete, and, thus, I could not do triathlons, and that was the way it was.* Without questioning this Story, it hadn't even occurred to me that—duh—no one was *born* an athlete. Every athlete who has ever existed *became one* because they put time into training.

This shift in my thinking is exactly what it looks like to examine your limiting Stories and "reframe" them. Even when we start accessing the body and questioning the power of the Critic, there's still work to be done when we haven't yet uncovered our limiting assumptions about ourselves or when we assume that we can't do something because that's just "the way it is."

Remember Alexis from the Introduction, a project manager who wanted to bring some heart into corporate America? She told me that if she tried to bring heart-based communication into the workplace, she'd "be laughed out of the boardroom." What was her Story? *Corporate America isn't interested in heart-based communication. That's just the way corporate America is, right?* Shay, a badass yoga instructor in a moto jacket redefined what her most courageous self was capable of when she questioned her Story that yoga teachers were supposed to only offer a gentle, breathy "Namaste." *That's just the way yoga teachers operate, right?* Janelle, mother of three, had to unhook from her Story that *good moms did things a certain way—the endlessly self-sacrificing way.* Eliana, MBA candidate who checked and double-checked her work to the point of being overwhelmed, had to unhook from the Story that she *couldn't make mistakes.* Taylor had to unhook from the Story that she *wasn't good enough or talented enough to make self-employment happen.*

If we assume our limiting Stories are true, we will continue to limit what we believe we are capable of. Unhooking from limiting Stories doesn't happen by reciting uber-positive "affirmations" that are out of touch with reality, and hoping for the best. Instead, reframing limiting Stories happens when we question assumed beliefs about "the way it is," and then choose a different Story, one that expands and builds resilience.

Often, we forget that it takes just as much effort to believe that your dreams aren't possible as it does to believe that what you want can be created. It's absolutely possible to consciously choose your Stories. Choosing Stories such as *I'm capable of recovering from a setback, I'm willing to meet this challenge,* or *I refuse to give up hope* will build resilience as you encounter fear, setbacks, self-doubt, or challenges.

It's time for step three of the Courage Habit: reframing limiting Stories. To do this, you'll first learn what Stories are and uncover any limiting Stories that you currently hold, bringing to light any assumptions about what you're capable of creating. After that, you'll learn how to reframe limiting Stories and instead choose Stories that expand your view of what's possible.

What Are Stories?

Stories are internal narratives and assumptions that we make about how the world operates. But, here's the important part: Stories might not be *objectively* true. They are your lens on life and, like a pair of sunglasses, can change how you see the world. The Story you put on your experience has everything to do with whether you see yourself as a victim or a survivor, whether an experience is dangerous or an opportunity, and whether you have the capacity to develop more courage or if you are *just not very courageous.*

It's not wrong to adopt Stories. Everyone's got internal assumptions that we use to orient ourselves in the world, but some Stories are more *helpful* than others. For instance, we've probably all met people who carry a Story that *everyone is selfish and only out for themselves.* Because these people carry that Story, they are suspicious of other people's motives, inclined to tally up other people's wrongs, and have a "gotta look out for myself" attitude. When it comes to living a happy life, that Story probably isn't very helpful.

We've also all probably all met people who carry a Story that *everyone is kind and doing the best they can.* Because these people carry that Story, they probably give others the benefit of the doubt, take things less personally, and see other people as interdependent. That Story is much more helpful.

These two Stories color the entire outlook of people who carry them, and affect how they view the world and interact with other human beings. A person can certainly function in life with both Stories. However, if you were the person who felt stuck in believing that everyone's selfish and out for themselves, wouldn't you be grateful if someone could help you unhook from that story and believe that the world is full of people who are kind and do the best they can?

That's exactly why it's important to examine the Stories that we inherently assume to be true. We might carry some that are limiting, just as I did when I was dismissing the idea of becoming a triathlete, or as Shay did when she taught yoga classes like she was "supposed to," or as Janelle did when she assumed a predetermined role of "how mothers behave" and acted accordingly.

Sometimes people ask me if it's possible to change their Stories. My answer? I've seen time and again that it is possible to consciously choose your Stories. Consciously choosing your Stories is a matter of where you put your attention and what you decide to make things mean.

Carolyn

Carolyn, tall and willowy like a model, was the very definition of a quintessential California free spirit. She and I met at a yoga workshop where our mats ended up side by side. We hit it off, talking during breaks and downward dog when the teacher wasn't looking, giving the backstory behind each of our tattoos, and making plans to see Ani DiFranco live. Carolyn didn't live nearby. When I asked where she was from, she replied with a shrug, "everywhere," and proceeded to tell me about the nomadic lifestyle that she had set up for herself.

"I couch surf. I do some trade. Freedom. I go wherever I'm called to go," she said. "I came to the San Francisco area a few months ago when I met this guy named Paris. He is a metal worker, and is into aerial arts. He was doing this festival thing down in Oakland, so I stayed with him for a while. His roommate Keri was heading up here for this yoga workshop. She's friends with the teacher and could get me a free spot. So, I came up here."

I couldn't help but feel a bit envious of Carolyn's freedom, and at the same time I couldn't help but think of the logistics. "How do you make money moving around so much?" I asked.

Carolyn smiled and her fingers played with a crystal around her neck. "It just always works out," she said. "I know how to code websites. You can do it from anywhere, you know? What I'd really love to do is what you do—coaching people. That sounds so rad. Maybe you should be my coach. I could use some more courage."

I laughed. I rarely heard anyone describe coaching as "rad." Carolyn seemed pretty courageous to me, exactly like someone who was living fully from the place of her most courageous self. What would she even want to work on? But, after talking for a bit and hearing that I might need some website work, Carolyn had a proposal for me. "How about we trade hours of coaching for hours of website work?" I was game to try it, especially since my website needed an upgrade.

A few weeks later, we were set up for our first session. Carolyn called in from Oregon where she was staying with a childhood friend who lived there. She had sent me some presession questions prior to our session. In the section where I had asked what it was that she wanted to gain from coaching, she wrote, simply: "Get out of debt."

On the phone, after we exchanged a few hellos, I asked her to tell me more about the debt so that I could get a clear picture of what was going on. The lighthearted "it just always works out" Carolyn was suddenly gone. Her voice wavered; she whispered so softly I had to ask her to repeat herself. "I've got $60,000 in debt," she whispered, hardly getting the words out. She proceeded to tell me about student loans she'd defaulted on after her mother got sick with pancreatic cancer several years before. Her father had never been in the picture, so he wasn't a resource she could lean on. She'd dropped out of school to care for her mother and racked up a small fortune in credit card debt. In trying to keep up with the payments on those bills, she'd fallen behind on her tax payments. The most difficult year of her life, with her mother's death and the debt she incurred, had become a total financial meltdown that rolled from one year to the next, and she could never seem to get ahead.

I was starting to get a bigger picture of Carolyn's nomadic lifestyle as being not so much about freedom as it was about running. As it turned out, Carolyn moved around so much because she couldn't pass a credit check to rent an apartment. She traded her website work for the things she needed because the IRS would garnish any wages that she earned from traditional employment. The result? Carolyn was frequently hit with insomnia when she thought about the debt. On two occasions, she'd had extreme panic attacks. Without a job or health insurance, she had ended up in the emergency room multiple times, incurring even more debt.

"The nomad thing is just something I say," Carolyn confessed. "I guess that makes it light and happy, and, you know, easier. Because the truth just totally sucks. Like, I have no idea how I'm going to have dinner tonight. Usually I can figure out some way to trade something or I'll just go without dinner one night, but it feels so lame. My mother would be so pissed at me if she saw me living like this. This wasn't what she wanted for me. I wish I just had something stable—one place to live, one job to go to. You know, a normal life."

I'd had no idea that Carolyn was carrying all this. She wasn't technically "homeless," since thus far she'd always found somewhere to stay. However, she once had to leave the house of a guy "friend" who thought that if he gave her a place to stay for the night, she would have sex with him. Carolyn was highly resourceful, but also becoming exhausted by this lifestyle.

As we finished our first session, we talked about the tool of accessing the body, a highly practical one for someone who was carrying as much as Carolyn was carrying. Then, I added that from a purely strategic place, it sounded like Carolyn needed to take two big actions before our next session. First, she needed to learn more about what options were available to someone in her situation. Second, she needed to start thinking about how to create stability.

"You said you wanted one place to live, and one job to go to," I said. "So, start thinking through your options. What's the easiest route to that?"

When we hopped off the phone that day, Carolyn sounded like she was doing better. "I'm feeling a bit better," she said, "I feel like I've got the start of a plan. I'm going to go to the library and start looking at jobs as soon as we're off the phone." The power of what Story we choose was evident. Carolyn noticed that the Story *I've got the start of a plan* was making her feel more hopeful and optimistic.

In the weeks of coaching that followed, it quickly became evident that Carolyn's fear routine involved self-sabotage, and she was a classic Saboteur. Even before her mother became sick, Carolyn had struggled to choose a major in college, deferring the decision as long as possible until she finally chose her major. Later, after she'd already declared, she petitioned the college board for a special exception allowing her to change majors. By age thirty, she'd already received three marriage proposals, two of which she had accepted and started planning the wedding for before she called them off. We started talking about the behaviors that go along with self-sabotage. Was she aware of them? "Totally," she said. "I feel like all my teachers ever said to me growing up was that I had good potential if I would only apply myself."

Carolyn was a lot of things—smart, creative, incredibly resourceful, and in so many ways she had the kind of courage that the rest of us admire. Yes, she had trouble with commitment, but she was a fundamentally good person who was pretty universally adored, as evidenced by a wide network of friends who would let her crash with them on a moment's notice. She wanted to change, but she just didn't know how to yet. Identifying, questioning, and reframing her biggest limiting Story would prove to be what changed everything.

Identifying Limiting Stories

Think back to Chapter 1 and the routines of the Perfectionist, Saboteur, Martyr, and Pessimist. In the cue-routine-reward loop that underlies all our habits, the Stories we assume to be true will parallel someone's fear routine. If you've got a fear routine as a Martyr, your Stories are likely to be things like *I should make sure that everyone else is happy.* If you've got a fear routine as a Perfectionist, your Stories are likely to be things like *I've got to work harder; this isn't good enough, yet!* If you've got a fear routine as a Pessimist, your Stories are likely to be *There's no point in trying.* For the exercises in this chapter, keep in mind the connection between your most dominant fear routine and the Stories that you tend to hold.

For a Saboteur such as Carolyn, I was on the lookout for Stories that had to do with sabotaging legitimate possibilities. I noticed that she was starting to show up just a little late to our session calls, and more frequently she was not completing all the practices between our sessions.

"You get to decide what it means," I said, when I brought up what I'd noticed. Then, there was a session when she arrived really late, keeping me waiting. "I want to support you in shifting by pointing out that a lack of commitment to a process is part of the Saboteur routine," I said, wanting to point out what I saw without going into a space of admonishing her.

"Look," she said abruptly, "The thing is, I got offered a job." Then, she added, with a voice that was tense and defensive, "And, I'm *not* taking it. There's no way. I just wanted to let you know."

At first, I didn't know what to say, and Carolyn was a little clipped with the details. However, the details eventually came out. A friend of hers had recently been promoted at a tech company in Seattle and was offering Carolyn a job there. The salary? More than a $100,000 a year, plus they would put Carolyn up in a condo for sixty days while she searched for a rental in Seattle's tight rental market. Nonetheless, Carolyn was clearly not happy about it.

"Okay," I said slowly, trying to think my way through the situation. I wanted Carolyn to feel that I was supportive of her choices, and she clearly didn't want to take this job. At the same time, Carolyn had never expressed feeling good about the financial insecurity that she was in, and with no other jobs knocking at her door with six-figure salaries, what was she going to do? Finally, I asked her if she was willing to try laying out all her options on the table—even the ones that she didn't love.

"Well, one option is I keep doing what I'm doing," Carolyn said. "I think that that's the best option for right now. I'm finishing up staying in Oregon this week, and then I think I'm going to talk to a cousin of mine in Colorado who is having her first baby soon and see if it's okay for me to stay with her and her husband and help them out with the baby."

"Okay, what else?" I asked.

Carolyn paused for a long time before she answered. "Another option is taking this job, but that's not really an option," Carolyn finally said, sounding defensive again.

"Why not?" I asked.

"It's just…I just know that it's all wrong for me," Carolyn said. "I see how my friend is living, the one doing the hiring. She's married to her work. I see how everyone lives in these stupid corporate jobs. They just work, and then they buy houses and get tied to mortgages, and the highlight of their day is coming home to open a bottle of wine. I'm not down with that. That's not me."

"But wait," I countered. "How did we get from taking a job to *My life becomes nothing but work and a mortgage and dependence on alcohol?*"

"That's just the way it is," Carolyn said, and I heard emotion coming into her voice. "You start settling for one option, and your life is over."

As we talked, I realized that this was Carolyn's capital-S Story: *Committing to one option means you're settling, and then you never get to have fun anymore.* That's why it had been difficult to commit to a major in school, or a partner in life, and why she was having trouble with the idea of this job. Commitment, for Carolyn, meant feeling tied down. Being in debt and floating around was scary, in its own way, but not as terrifying as commitment. That's why Carolyn had made so many moves that had taken her two steps forward, only to take one step back.

I felt nervous as I shared these thoughts with Carolyn. She'd seemed so annoyed with me from the get-go on this call, which I now suspected was because she knew, deep down, that I would call her out on her behavior.

"What do you think?" I asked after I shared what I'd noticed. After a long silence, Carolyn finally agreed that she'd think about it. We ended that day's session early, and I hung up the phone wondering where our work together would go next, or if it would even continue.

Carolyn's Story that *Commitment means settling, and then you never have fun* was protecting her from facing her fear of sticking with one thing and really learning how to *just stay* with what she had chosen. She believed in herself and her capability enough to start down a particular avenue, but then that Saboteur Story about commitment, which seemed so obvious to Carolyn, would crop up.

Again, these Stories are protective mechanisms that are parallel to our fear routines. The Martyr uses the Story of *I've got to make sure that everyone else is happy* as a form of protection. If she's always running around making sure everyone else is happy, then she doesn't have time for living her own life and experiencing the vulnerability that comes with naming what she desires or pursuing it. The Pessimist uses the Story *Things never seem to work out for me* as a protection from the pain of possible failure. The Perfectionist is doing the same thing, in a different way, using the Story of *I've got to work harder* and endlessly pushing herself to be better to avoid experiencing criticism and the risk of failure.

Since our Stories are based in our assumptions and beliefs about who we are and the way the world works, they can operate in ways that can be difficult to recognize. Deciding to tune in to the Critic after years of regarding it as background noise, you might not even realize that you've been basing some of your choices on assumed Stories.

Within an hour after ending our session, I received an email from Carolyn. It read: "I thought about it, and I think you're right about the Story I carry. But, now what?"

I hit reply, and typed back: "We—you—get to change the Story."

Bringing Stories to your consciousness and reframing them so that you see your life differently is an empowering act. If you're out walking on a forest trail and see something coiled up on the path up ahead, it's helpful that your body responds immediately to see that there could be danger. Rather than not walking down that path and remaining avoidant or afraid, make sure you know whether what's coiled ahead is a snake or a rope. If you look a little closer at the thing that you fear and see that it's just a rope, you can't go back to seeing a snake. That's what it's like to get out from under a limiting Story based in old fear routines.

Identifying Your Stories

Let's do a deep dive into uncovering some of your own Stories. For this exercise, use a journal or piece of paper to answer the questions that follow. You can also download the "Identifying Your Stories" worksheet at http://www.yourcourageouslife.com /courage-habit, if you prefer.

1. First, think of an aspect of your Primary Focus or of stepping into your most courageous self where you've felt a little bit stuck. It could be feeling a lack of resources, a sense of confusion, or difficulties with the Inner Critic. Try to see yourself in that place of being stuck, only for a moment. Now, finish the following sentences:

    I'm frustrated because...

    I wish _____ would stop...

    This feels so difficult because...

    Then, stop. Breathe. Remember to access the body.

2.   What does your Critic say about your progress? Write it down.

> My Critic says I *should* be...
>
> My Critic says I *shouldn't* be...

3.   To tease out what Stories you might be telling yourself, finish these sentences:

> With my Primary Focus, I feel like I need to do/be more...
>
> With my most courageous self, I feel like I can't...
>
> With my Primary Focus, I never have enough _____ or feel _____ enough.
>
> To change my life, I don't know...

4.   When it comes to my big dreams or living fully as my most courageous self, I think...

After completing the exercise, review your answers and then create a list of all the possible Stories that you can identify. As you're making this list, a part of you might rebel. It might jump in and say, "No, wait! You don't believe that to be true. You're more powerful than that; don't write that down." While it's great that this more courageous part of yourself is stepping up and making itself known, the value in this exercise is in getting real about the Stories that hold you back. To reframe limiting Stories, start with writing down *exactly* how the Story sounds in your head when you're in a fear routine. Don't edit yourself before you fully explore the Stories that play out; it's likely to result in the same Story creeping back up, time and time again.

Common Stories of Limitation

As part of uncovering Stories, I frequently ask clients to pay attention to the three most common areas where people hold Stories of limitation. If you scan your own list of Stories you came up with from the last exercise, you'll probably find that you have Stories that are related to one of the following three categories:

Stories of how we were raised. This is the Story of the past—the parents who were more interested in their addictions than in raising children, the teachers who told you that you wouldn't amount to anything, and the culture that encouraged you to be quiet and not say what you really think.

Stories about circumstances. These are Stories about tough external circumstances limiting progress, such as not having enough time, money, or support for your ideas. Thinking that you're "too busy" and will get to it later is another Story of circumstance.

Stories about what's possible. These are the Stories about an inherent, unalterable lack of capability, or an assumption that things inevitably won't work out before there's any indication that this would be true. *I'm not smart or talented enough. Someone else has already done it, so I shouldn't bother. I'd never finish anyway. No one cares about that but me. I'm too young/old. The moment has passed.*

Review your list of Stories from the "Identifying Your Stories" exercise, and put a star next to any of the Stories that fall into one of these categories. These types of Stories are among the most powerful ones that hold sway over our ideas about how possible change really is. These Stories come from very real and painful past experiences that I wouldn't want you to deny, bypass, or gloss over. Parents abuse children, discrimination is real and leaves an impact, and lack of time and money are not just individual concerns but also reflections of systemic inequalities in our culture. Even though those challenges are very real, the idea here is to see where Stories of limitation enter the picture so that those Stories can be reckoned with, understood, and acknowledged so they no longer dominate your life. Rather than pretend that a painful past didn't happen or that everything in the future will always be easy, reframing limiting Stories helps you to pragmatically address where you limit yourself, and pushes you to see what's possible even if that's hard to imagine. That was what happened in the past, and now you can expand your ideas about how you want to live in the present moment.

Questioning Our Limiting Stories

When we uncover our limiting and unhelpful Stories, we have an opportunity to choose the next direction of our lives through asking ourselves: "Do I truly believe this Story?" Answering that question can be incredibly powerful, especially if you realize that there's ample evidence supporting a different, more positive narrative for your life.

Carolyn had a limited amount of time to decide about the job offer she'd been given, as her friend needed to fill the position right away. That week, we scheduled an extra session and did a deep dive into examining Carolyn's Story, holding it up to the light of her truth. *Commitment to one thing means settling—and then you never have fun anymore.* Was that true?

Carolyn logically realized that this Story wasn't *absolutely* true. Even if it was true for some people, it didn't need to be for her. We began talking about assumptions. Commitment could mean a lot of things, so what did Carolyn assume commitment had to mean for her? If she questioned the assumptions she'd been carrying about what "commitment" meant and tried out alternative ideas, she could ask herself: *What does commitment mean for me? What are the parameters? How long did commitment have to last? What was acceptable and what* wasn't?

"I just realized one other thing," Carolyn said as we talked about the Stories of circumstances of how we were raised and of what's possible. "My story is tied to what's possible. I fundamentally don't see myself as someone who is 'a commitment person.' It's like I have this idea in my head that there are two types of people in the world, and I'm just not one of those 'commitment people.' I've always thought it was no big deal, because who was I hurting?"

"That's brilliant of you to notice," I said. "Have you hurt anyone?"

"Well, yeah—Charlie and Wyatt," Carolyn said, naming the two men she had accepted proposals from and ultimately broken up with. "They didn't know that I was saying yes to the commitment, before I actually felt *able* to make the commitment. And, given that I'm not actually happy...I've been hurting myself by bailing, over and over. I just keep feeling this impulse to run to the next thing, and I follow it in the moment, but that's my fear routine, not what I really want."

I encouraged Carolyn to get every single Story—positive or negative—about accepting this job out onto the table. Yes, this job could cover Carolyn's expenses and get her out of debt, but we both knew that if she accepted it without really being fully behind that choice it would be just another thing that she started but didn't follow through on. We wanted to examine every Story on her list, and really look at them thoroughly, turning them over and questioning them.

I encourage you to do the same, creating an exhaustive list and really questioning each Story that might hold you back. Take time now to revisit the list of Stories that you've already identified. Ask yourself, "What am I making this mean?" and "Is this really true?"

As an example, this chapter started with my own Story that I wasn't an athlete. The underlying Story was that I was fundamentally unable to become one—a Story of limitation about what was possible.

"What am I making this mean?" *That I'm not capable of completing a triathlon.*

"Is this really true?" *No. If I put the time in, I can probably complete a triathlon.*

Here's another example: Janelle, the mother of three from an earlier chapter, had the Story that *a good mother is self-sacrificing.*

"What am I making this mean?" *That unless I'm self-sacrificing, I must be a bad mother.*

"Is this really true?" *Not unless I believe it is. I can define what it means for me to be a good mother.*

Apply this same process to your own list of Stories. For each Story on the list, ask yourself "What am I making this mean?" and "Is this really true?" Write down your responses as you go and hold on to what you write, because now it's time to start reframing limiting Stories.

Reframing Limiting Stories

In the last section, you questioned some of your limiting Stories and started to see how they might not have stood up to the light of your truth. As you embark on the process of reframing your Stories, you'll be making a conscious choice to release a limiting, constrictive Story for a more resilient, expansive Story. When I explained this to Carolyn, she said, "Wait. Are these affirmations? I *hate* positive affirmations."

"Oh, good. Me, too," I said. While "positive affirmations" are pervasive among coaches, I'm truly not a fan. I've lost count of how many people have told me that they chafe at the idea of reciting them, too. This isn't an aversion based on an inherent or stuck negativity. Most of us have tried reciting affirmations—with some doggedness—only to feel frustrated, like we've just been lying to ourselves, over and over. Positive affirmations are based on pushing yourself to believe something wildly optimistic that may or may not be possible, and they involve bypassing any acknowledgment of "negative" feelings, such as fear. If Carolyn wanted to, for instance, get rid of her credit card debt, I didn't think the answer was to say, "I'm a multimillionaire!" or "I'm debt-free!" until she was out of breath.

Even worse, asking people to focus on positive affirmations when they're dealing with oppression (such as discrimination based on race, sexual orientation, and gender; a traumatic upbringing; or a systemic lack of access to money or resources) lacks empathy for the very real suffering and impact of those experiences. Carolyn fell into that category, given her lack of financial capital in a society that offers very little in the way of a safety net. This made her vulnerable to accruing debt that she would have trouble ever paying back.

The bottom line is that the hurts that we have survived or that we are still trying to survive are very real. The conditioning that you grew up with is not "just in your head," nor is change just a matter of only thinking positive thoughts. In reframing limiting Stories, we're not trying to brush over past experiences of oppression or the effects of our conditioning. In exploring and dismantling limiting Stories, our aim is to stop these Stories from running on a continuous, endless loop that limits our life, in which the pain gets revisited and there is no resolution.

Choosing to find the positive amid difficult circumstances is the real aim. Hard things and serious life challenges still happen to people who consciously choose more positive Stories. What you find when you start to reframe is that the choice to continually look for a more positive Story is part of a resilience strategy to bounce back from those difficulties. Examining your Stories so that you can consciously choose those that are more positive or supportive of your goals isn't naïve. In being willing to believe that options are available, you're more likely to find them. Think of reframing limiting Stories as a process of releasing limiting beliefs that may be illusory rather than real, and stretching into the direction of more courageous and fulfilling options. Acknowledge what might be old or part of your past and where you are in the here and now, then see where you can stretch in a more helpful direction.

With Carolyn, this started with taking statements from her list of Stories, one by one, and reframing them. She found that one of her Stories about debt was *This is so big and I'll never pay it off.* This was a way of thinking about her life that sometimes caused her to spend unwisely, given her financial situation. A Story that rationalized such moments was *Since I'll never get ahead, I might as well have a little fun where I can.* She reframed that with the statement *I'm committed to paying this off, even if all I can afford to pay is the monthly minimums.* She wasn't wildly declaring that she'd be a millionaire or pretending that the debt was going to be gone overnight. She was declaring her commitment to shifting her circumstances.

When it came to her Story about commitment being all about settling, Carolyn started with *I get to define what commitment means, and whether or not I'm settling.* She wasn't trying to pretend with the snap of her fingers that she no longer believed that commitment and settling were intertwined. Rather, she was reframing in the direction of what she wanted, starting with acknowledging that she could define for herself what commitment would mean to her.

Reframing Your Stories

To reframe a Story, start with what's authentically true. (*In this moment, I'm in debt.*) Then, stretch it in a more positive direction. (*In this moment, I'm in debt, and I'm determined to change that.*) It's the combination of what is true *and* a more positive stretch that is important. Try your hand at reframing some of the Stories that you've questioned. The questioning process might have turned up some potential reframes. There's also a worksheet for writing down your reframes at http://www.yourcourageouslife.com/courage-habit.

The following example is another way to think about potential reframes and how you might move through the process. Read through each reframe below for the Story example of *I'm not capable of doing this.* Each new statement is an example of stretching the Story in a slightly more positive direction.

I'm not capable of doing this.

↓

I'm willing to look at my options.

↓

If I put time into this, I think I could get capable.

↓

I'm choosing to take action with one option.

↓

I'm willing to get consistent with taking action.

↓

I am getting consistent with taking action.

When I questioned and reframed my Story that I wasn't a "real" athlete, I initially shifted to, *Well, I could try and see what happens.* Then, that Story became *I'm not fast at swimming, cycling, or running, but I'm able to be consistent with my training.* Then, that Story became *I can finish a short-distance triathlon!* Each Story built on the next, in a more positive direction.

Within a year after doing my first short "sprint" triathlon, I completed a half-Ironman triathlon: a 1.2-mile swim, followed by 56 miles on the bike, and finishing with a 13.1-mile run. It took more than eight hours to complete, but the bigger journey was the shift from "I can't" to "I can." I never could have jumped straight from *I'm not an athlete* to *I'm a half-Ironman finisher.* Noticing every limiting Story along the way, and consciously reframing each Story as it came up, was key.

Now that you've seen a few examples, try reframing some Stories yourself. Take each sentence, one at a time, and reframe it. Keep the authentic truth, and stretch it in a more positive direction.

Write down three different Stories from the "Identifying Your Stories" exercise here:

1. _____

2. _____

3. _____

Now, work with just one Story at a time. Keep repeating the process of stretching in a more positive direction until you hit that point where you know that going any further would feel more "fake" than like a reframe.

Story #1: _____

If I stretch just ONE step in a more positive direction, this Story becomes: _____

Now, try stretching the above sentence, again, just one step more in a positive direction: _____

Try stretching the above sentence, just one more step:

_____

Repeat these small stretches until you've arrived at a reframed Story that you can authentically embrace. Repeat each of these steps for the other Stories that you wrote down, or any time you notice that limiting Stories have you feeling stuck.

What happens after you've reframed your Stories? How do you turn these reframes into actions that make your daily life any different? Once you've reframed any Story, you start reminding yourself of your *choice* to believe something different. You get to decide which Story you want to choose. Awareness of your existing limiting Stories and your desired reframes becomes something that you're more present to when the Stories arise. Being present with your Stories is ongoing work, but as you stretch one small step in the direction of your most courageous self, you'll find that changing your Stories is happening organically, one small shift at a time.

Putting the Pieces Together

Carolyn had a big decision to make with this job. We uncovered her Stories and went through the Courage Habit steps during a few intensive sessions. Through accessing the body, she tried to notice that moment when her fear routine wanted to kick in, encouraging her to run from her debt problems and keep doing what she'd been doing only because it was familiar. She tried to notice the Critic who told her it was no big deal to bail on a commitment and then would criticize her later for that choice. Most of all, she paid attention to the limiting Stories and assumptions she'd made about commitment that had made it easier to rationalize quitting.

Carolyn eventually decided to take the job. We had sessions for a few more months while she got settled in Seattle. Her life got busy and she felt more grounded in the new life she was creating, so we discontinued sessions, and over time lost touch. Then, a few years later, I was heading into yoga, and there was Carolyn, who happened to be visiting my town. We hugged excitedly, and after class we decided to grab an impromptu dinner and catch up.

"So how are things?" I asked, trying to mask a raging curiosity because I didn't want it to seem like I was prying. Carolyn didn't need much encouragement; she was happy to give me an update. She'd had a few bumps and U-turns on her journey, but she had stayed the course and finally paid down all her debt. She now fed her wanderlust with accrued paid-vacation time! She admitted that sometimes she felt like she couldn't be as spontaneous as she wanted to be. Instead of feeling trapped by that feeling, she tried to question the Story that she was "trapped" and then find some other way to break out of her usual day-to-day routines, such as taking a spontaneous "sick day" and staying home to do whatever she felt like doing.

"I find if I break the rules just a little bit, the part of me that wants to completely throw the rules out gets what it needs," she confessed. She also had met someone, a man named Gregory, and they had been dating for a little more than a year.

The woman I saw before me was living with a different kind of freedom. What Carolyn had called "freedom" when I first met her had looked courageous on the outside, but it was really a life built on fear and hiding from facing her debt or making decisions about what she wanted for her life. This Carolyn was a different person, someone who had faced her fears and created freedom through powerfully making decisions. That included choosing which Stories about herself she wanted to believe. Her old, fear-based Story was that *being committed to a job would mean feeling trapped.* Her more expansive Story became: *This job gives me more freedom, even if it also comes with responsibility.*

Being willing to identify your limiting Stories, question them, and then reframe them, is a game changer. This is where you start seeing the power that you've always held to create what you've always wanted. Changing old, fear-based habits and ways of thinking is possible.

Moving Forward

By now, you're probably seeing how each part of the Courage Habit process provides reinforcement for the other parts. Stopping and slowing down to access the body is a first step, so that you can be present to the fear sensations that you feel and be mindful of not going into a fear routine on autopilot. From there, you listen to your Critic voices without attachment, which clues you in to what sort of fears are aroused. After that, seeing and consciously reframing those Stories gives you another powerful tool.

There's only one more part of the Courage Habit process. It's a step that research has shown to be one of the most influential in solidifying newly established habits. This step helps you to practice these tools in a larger context, outside of yourself. This step is also one of the most fun: It's about reaching out and creating community.

Chapter 6

Reach Out and Create Community

For all my courageous dreaming, the very first time that I led an online course to teach people how to practice more courage in their lives, things didn't go as well as I'd hoped. It all started out great—sixty people from the United States and various other countries signed up for the course! As people began to make their first introductions in our private online forums, I found that I'd go to bed at night unable to sleep because I was so excited about all that would await us. I was running a course and growing my business, while doing work that I loved and believed in!

My enthusiasm (and my ego) were delivered something of a shock when, about a week into the course, participation began to taper off. By the end of the second week, only about half of the participants were posting their thoughts about the lessons in our group forum. Instead, they were emailing me one-on-one to talk about the lessons, which was fine, but hardly the community-focused, enthusiastic group discussion I'd intended.

Then, something happened that really threw me into a tail-spin. Someone emailed me three weeks into the course to ask for a refund. I immediately assumed that it must be that I wasn't running the course well enough, and that my inability to create more group connection was the cause (notice the *I'm not enough Story*). My fear and insecurity went into overdrive as I obsessed over everything that I was doing, should have been doing, or could have done. When the course ended eight weeks later, my insecurity about the lack of participation was so intense that I was relieved the course was over.

Here I was, the person who was supposed to be practicing so much courage, and yet if I was honest, I felt like a failure. The participants of my course hadn't seemed to connect with one another. I was scared to run another course. I'd taken a leave of absence from my job and was living off my savings and quickly accruing credit card debt. In the movies, taking risks was always rewarded, so why wasn't this working out as I'd planned?

Weeks later, a friend named McCabe, a woman who had been running courses and workshops for years, visited San Francisco. We spent a day walking around San Francisco and taking photos. Later, we stopped to have tea in Chinatown, and she asked how things had been going. I took a deep breath.

"I keep trying to stay positive, but I feel like an idiot for thinking that this working for myself thing would ever work," I told her. As bad as it felt to say that, there was a part of me that felt almost relieved. *Finally, the truth.* I told her about the lackluster participation and how afraid I was.

"Wait a sec, Kate," McCabe said. "Walk me through this, again. How long did the course run, and what were the numbers for enrollment and participation?"

I said, "The course was eight weeks, and sixty people were there at the start. One person asked for a refund. About a third of the people never really participated at all. Some other people participated a bit more at the beginning, but then I felt like I hardly heard from them. The others mostly emailed me to talk about their individual progress in the course, rather than connecting as a group. I don't know what I did wrong. I kept encouraging people to share, but…"

"Hold on," McCabe said, her brow furrowed as she made some mental calculations. I waited, feeling some of my embarrassment return as I thought about how lack of sleep due to my excitement had turned into lack of sleep over how poorly things had gone. My Critic was loud: "I didn't know anything about running a business. I had no business experience. I'd just created this course on a whim of following my dreams and practicing courage, and look where it had gotten me."

"So, basically, you had a 2-percent refund rate?" McCabe said, interrupting my rumination now that she'd arrived at some fast calculations. "And, you said one-third didn't really participate, so two-thirds of the participants were participating, so at least 66 percent of your participants were participating?"

"Well," I said, her words catching me off guard. "Yeah—it's just that most people weren't really participating as much in the whole group."

"Kate," McCabe said, grabbing my arm so that I'd look her in the eye. "I'm not, like, trying to downplay how you feel, here, but do you know how *good* those results are? The majority was participating, on some level. You know, not everyone participates in an outward, extroverted way. Maybe the only thing needed here is some work to learn how to help the group come together more cohesively. Maybe you had a group with a lot of introverts. *You did so well, Kate.* Only *one* person in the entire bunch requested a refund. I really want you to see that this is a success, especially for your first-ever time doing this."

It was taking me a minute to fully digest that my Perfectionist fear routine had been the one running the show the entire time, telling me Stories that I'd been believing about how much more should have been happening, and I hadn't realized it. McCabe had years of experience as a facilitator, and if anyone would know what made for a successful course, she would.

"But the people weren't really connected to one another," I said, struggling to square this new information with how real the feelings of failure felt. "How do you get your groups to do that?"

"First tell me this," McCabe said, "I'm sure that the lessons of courage that you teach are just as important for each individual as for a group who is connected to each other. So, why is it so impor- tant to you as a teacher that the participants are connected as a group? What's the lesson for them in that group connection?"

For a moment, I struggled to articulate what I knew to be so true inside, and then I found the words. "It's important to connect with other people who are trying to practice courage for the same reason that we're talking right now, because when you have a hard time and feel alone, you need to know that there are other people who 'get it.' And, when you have something great happen, it just doesn't feel as good to celebrate alone or with people who don't really understand what you're doing as it is to celebrate with someone who knows exactly how hard you worked to get there."

"From what you've told me," McCabe said, "People didn't turn to one another in this group because you personally were supplying their needs for support when they emailed you. You were the person they could turn to when it was hard, or when they were celebrating. So, next time you run the course, maybe you'll do a bit more to get people to connect with each other. But, Kate, you did your job as the teacher. You showed up for the people who were willing to do the work, even if it didn't go as you'd planned."

Talk about the teacher needing to learn her own lessons! That day, I realized that I *myself* had been hesitating to reach out, perhaps even in the same way some of the participants had been hesitating. My fear routine perpetuated itself *without my awareness*. Even with all the work that I did on my own to try to be self-aware, a fear routine could still hook me.

To truly live courageous lives, we need other like-minded people around us who are also trying to honor the values of courage. Why do we need this? First, creating courageous communities in our lives gives us the support we need to face challenges. Sometimes we just don't see what's right in front of us, and we need people who are doing similar work to help us to see the truth, as McCabe did for me. Most of all, you need to know who is in your own personal "courageous community." When it's time to celebrate, it's just so much more *fun* to do it with people who have been with you through all the ups and downs, rough days, and victories. Talking to someone about your experience who truly "gets it" is far more satisfying. Quite simply, reaching out and creating community is part of living a better life.

The research into habit-formation also confirms the need for social support. Charles Duhigg, author of *The Power of Habit* (2014), writes: "For most people who overhaul their lives, there are no seminal moments or life-altering disasters. There are simply communities—sometimes of just one other person—who make change believable." He writes about a 1994 Harvard study in which participants found that being involved in a social group made change easier. "One woman said her entire life shifted when she signed up for a psychology class and met a wonderful group. 'It opened up a Pandora's box,' the woman told researchers. 'I could not tolerate the status quo any longer. I had changed my core.'"

The work you're doing with the Courage Habit is about no longer tolerating the status quo of a life lived with self-doubt or hesitation. You *are* changing at your core. You defined your Primary Focus and most courageous self, and then you began rerouting old habit loops, embarking on an entirely new path for your life. Everything you've done up to this point, with defining your most courageous self, then accessing the body and listening without attachment so that you could reframe limiting Stories, has primed you for this moment.

Creating courageous communities that support your changes will make the change not just believable, it'll make change truly possible. To do that, we'll start by looking at the qualities that underlie "courage-based" relationships, and from there we'll see how the first three parts of the Courage Habit can be applied to creating more connection in your life. We'll also address how to unhook from being negatively influenced by the people in your life who are unsupportive of the changes you're trying to make.

Creating Courage-Based Relationships

When I talk about "reaching out and creating community" as the fourth Courage Habit step, I'm talking about identifying or creating intentional relationships that support your bold dreams and desires for change. This means actively strengthening existing connections, as well as seeking out new connections that reflect where we are at in our lives. Shasta Nelson, a friendship expert and author of *Friendships Don't Just Happen!* (2013) writes, "The truth is that we all need to be constantly replenishing our circle of friends to ensure that it's meaningful for who we are, now."

The people who make up your courageous community might not be located near you nor even know one another. They won't be considered your "community" because they all get together in one large group. Rather, your personal community consists of your network of courage-based relationships in which people actively practice courage and work through fear by reaching out to one another and offering or receiving support.

In courage-based relationships, you aren't simply interacting with one another because it's convenient; you're being with one another in the *process* of practicing courage. If you consider the people you interact with on any given day, some of your existing relationships might already be courage based. Others may be more aptly described as "relationships of convenience." These would include family members you are not particularly close to but see over the holidays, the coworkers you get drinks with because you leave the office at the same time, or the moms you invite over mostly because your kids happen to get along. Everyone has relationships of convenience and they aren't bad, but they also aren't usually the relationships that you can truly lean on. The women you chat with at the gym might be good people who *interact* with you, but they aren't necessarily the people you bond with over the ups and downs, rough days, and victories of life.

To practice the Courage Habit step of reaching out and creating community, first you've got to know who you can reach out to. Where are the courage-based relationships in your life that will make up your courageous community? Who will be standing with you? Which relationships are courage based? Who is also playing the game of life from a place of taking risks in the name of their dreams, letting their most courageous selves emerge?

Who's in Your Corner?

Before you begin the following exercise, take a moment to breathe and access the body. Think of the people you interact with on a regular basis. Think about who you live with; who you work with; the people you run into at the grocery store, in volunteer groups, at church, in exercise classes; family members; and Internet communities. Then honestly ask yourself the question: Of these people, who is also trying to let their most courageous selves emerge alongside you? Go with your gut on this. Write down the names of the people who you sense (or see) going after something bigger in life. Maybe their goals aren't big and audacious, but you feel that there's something intentional, caring, and supportive about how they choose to live. Put down absolutely every name that you can think of.

Then, using this list of names, let's refine things to see who the star players are—the people who honor the value of courage through their way of being. Ask yourself if each person on your list practices any of the following "reaching out" behaviors that promote connection and support of one another. The examples below demonstrate what it looks like when people are reaching out in their own life. When they are reaching out, you'll hear them expressing:

- **Vulnerability Instead of Upholding an Image:** They'll admit when things are hard, instead of pretending that things are perfect.

- **Optimism Instead of Complaining:** While they're human and might sometimes need to vent and complain, in general they're hoping to find solutions to problems, rather than staying stuck in listing all the things that are wrong.

- **Empathy Instead of Advice:** When you talk about something that's upsetting, they offer understanding of how you feel, rather than listing suggestions for improvement.

- **Compassion over Critique:** They aren't gossiping, judging, or being catty about you or other people.

- **Kindness over Tough Love:** They will challenge you for your benefit in ways that are gentle and that you can hear, rather than harshly telling you to just get over your problems. For instance, McCabe was confronting me with kindness when she pointed out the ways in which my Stories had me hooked, but she didn't try to make me feel like an idiot because I hadn't realized sooner what was happening.

When you finish this exercise, you'll be looking at a list of people who might have very different personalities and might not be interested in the same topics or activities. However, they will have something in common: They practice the kind of "reaching out" behaviors that are essential to any tribe or community. Most of us appreciate those behaviors but take them for granted without really thinking, "Ah, I get it. These are my kind of people, and with their support I can make big changes in my life." You might not necessarily even be close to these people right now. That's okay. In this chapter, you'll see ways to start creating more connection with these individuals. You can also access this exercise at http://www.yourcourageouslife.com/courage-habit.

The first time I undertook this exercise, my own list of people who practiced the value of courage was painfully short. This exercise felt vulnerable to me, and the Story that came up was *I don't attract great people, because I'm not good enough for the great people to want to be around me.* After identifying the Story, I reframed it and reframed it and accepted that it might take time for me to strengthen existing relationships, or to meet new people who shared my values.

To strengthen relationships or meet more people who practice the value of courage, I had to look at myself and make sure that I was walking my talk. If I wanted courage-based relationships in which we mutually supported one another, I needed to start practicing the same "reaching out" behaviors that I was looking for. The people I practiced "reaching out" behaviors with would be the people who made up my personal courageous community. That community wasn't big at first. If that's the case for you, be willing to see this list grow, rather than getting stuck in disappointment.

Regardless of whether you think there are plenty of people to reach out to or no one fits the bill, the good news is that all the steps of the Courage Habit that you've been practicing thus far have paved the way for you to either strengthen your existing relationships or create new ones. The work starts in a familiar place. Practice the first three parts of the Courage Habit by accessing the body, listening without attachment, and reframing limiting Stories, *only this time* add the additional component of applying the first three Courage Habit parts as you practice "reaching out" behaviors.

For instance, if you want to meet new people and expand your community and you tend to be more introverted, you might feel nervous or be unsure of where to go to make new connections.

Try accessing the body, noting where fear sensations come up and do a body scan to see what your body has to say about your feelings of nervousness. Listen without attachment to the Critic who says that it's not going to go well or that you aren't social enough. Then, reframe those limiting Stories. If your Story is *I'm just not a very social person,* you could try *Even if I feel awkward being more social, I'm willing to step into some awkwardness.* In the actual moment of trying to be more social, if your Critic is critiquing how you are interacting, offer the Critic a silent "Re-do, please," and then internally reframe any Story that you're doing something badly. As you get to know a new person better, practice "reaching out" behaviors, such as offering compassion rather than critique or offering empathy rather than advice.

Let's say that you're more extroverted and have plenty of connections, but none of them feel particularly deep. Perhaps you have a family member you've often been in conflict with and you want that to shift. When interacting with this person, be open to sharing more about yourself from a heart-centered and vulnerable place, rather than sticking to easy and superficial topics of conversation. If you find that the person responds with some of that same vulnerability and courage, congrats! If he or she doesn't respond from that same open-hearted space, and you don't see the individual practicing other "reaching out" behaviors, note any limiting Stories that come up. Maybe the Stories are *Things will never change* or *I feel stupid for being vulnerable with her.* Reframe those Stories and be committed to finding others who are interested in "reaching out" behaviors.

All the Courage Habit steps support both your internal work to be more courageous and your external work to create more authentic, courage-based connections.

Making Connections

As I'm writing this chapter, I'm acutely aware that readers might fall into different camps. Some of you might feel like you've got plenty of support in your life, and thus these questions of how to get more support almost seem unnecessary. If that's you, I love the fact that you've got great connections as a resource in your life!

Other readers may feel more isolated in terms of those good, solid, and supportive connections. Maybe you were nodding your head as you read my earlier examples of "relationships of convenience." Perhaps you've always felt more introverted, or maybe you live in an area where there aren't as many like-minded people because there's a small population to choose from or because the general population seems to have drastically different interests or values.

Regardless of which camp you hail from, there's more connection available for you. Let's take a moment to go back to your Primary Focus and your desires for your most courageous self. Embedded within every desire that you have are opportunities for connecting with or creating a wider community. For some of you, bringing your Primary Focus to fruition will require that you get more connected with others. For example, if your deepest dream is to start a business, it will be essential to connect with people who know about business and marketing, not to mention you'll need the ability to connect with customers.

Pause for just a second and review your Primary Focus. How will more connection with people who are authentic, warm, and interested in creating courageous habits and lives help you? Perhaps write down next to each item on your Primary Focus the types of connection you'd like. When Janelle, the busy mom from earlier chapters, answered these questions, she realized that she was going to need to involve her husband if she wanted to relax her expectations of herself as a mother. When Taylor was answering these questions, she noted fellow photographers whom she had admired and wanted to befriend but was shy about reaching out to them.

To practice the Courage Habit step of reaching out and creating community, you'll need to actively practice reaching out, not just on paper but out in the real world. To see what that would look like, I'm going to ask you to choose a "practice person" whom you'll keep in mind both for the written exercises, as well as for your actual practice in the world. Taylor chose one specific photographer as her practice person for these exercises. Carolyn ended up doing her work around the father that had been largely absent during her life.

Take a moment to really solidify who that practice person will be, in your mind. Who would you like to be more connected to in your daily life? Or, who would you like to get to know better?

One quick note about resistance: It's highest when people feel most vulnerable, and relationships are a hot spot for feeling vulnerable. If you have any impulses to skip this chapter, or if there's suddenly a reason not to complete these exercises because they feel "too cheesy," then recognize this as your fear routine in action. Reaching out is the tool that really and truly brings all the Courage Habit steps together. Feeling weird, cheesy, a little anxious, or outright fearful is just part of the process, so keep the cue-routine-reward loop in mind and pay attention if this is the chapter where you start to go into a fear routine. You may want to revisit your goals for this work and the desires of your most courageous self to remind you of why it's so important to stay the course.

Connection and Accessing the Body

Start using the Courage Habit steps with relationships by accessing the body as an information-gathering way to notice what feels true or what your Critic says about your practice person. Take a no-pressure approach and start with just observing yourself as you think of your practice person—how you feel around this person and what you sense about him or her—while breathing and noticing what's arising in your body.

Initially, undertake this accessing the body without any initial intention of changing your behavior. You're just noticing. How is your breathing when you think of this practice person? Does your breathing change? How is your body? What do your shoulders or neck do when you imagine talking to this person about your goals and dreams? What happens in your body when you imagine listening to this person talking about her goals and dreams? Do you feel comfortable making eye contact with this person, or does that feel intimidating?

Notice feelings of curiosity, excitement, camaraderie, being fully seen, groundedness, relaxation, heaviness, tiredness, or anxiety. Just note them, write them down on a sheet of paper, and see what insights arise.

Connection and Listening Without Attachment

In an earlier chapter, you practiced the Courage Habit step of listening without attachment. With this process, you were intentional about noticing what your Critic had to say rather than trying to get it to go away, so that you could address its fears, insecurities, and wounds. Through listening to what it said without getting attached and not taking on the Critic's words as "truth," you could heal the Critic and stop getting stuck in its Stories.

Do the same thing with your practice person in mind. Check in to see if your Critic has anything to say about this individual, or about whether he or she would be a good person to get to know better. If there are fears about creating better connections or if your Critic has any critiques of you, get those out into the open. Write them down, and then use those statements in your work with part three: reframing limiting Stories.

Your Stories About Connection

After accessing the body and listening without attachment, the work shifts to noticing any internalized Stories that bar you from taking the actual step of reaching out. You've listened without attachment to what your Critic had to say, so what are the capital-S Stories? What are the critiques that keep you from feeling closer to this person and to other people? What are the limitations your Critic claims to be inherent within you, which leave you feeling silly or isolated?

Here are some common Stories that I've heard from clients that keep them from reaching out and being authentic about either their challenges or their celebrations:

I don't want to burden other people with my problems.

I feel weird and self-conscious when I get all bubbly and excited about something, so I usually make myself "calm down" before I'll share good news with other people.

They're just going to pity me. I hate it when other people pity me.

I'll feel stupid if they see just how messy my life is.

They'll think that who I am when I'm upset, stressed, and reaching out is who I am all the time.

I don't know if they'd accept me if I really told them the truth about who I am or how I feel.

They're going to see all the ways that I've screwed it up.

It's too embarrassing to open up and reveal more about myself, hear nothing but crickets, and feel like the people I just opened up to don't get it. I'm sure they wouldn't get it.

Remember that Stories are very, very convincing. They represent our assumptions and beliefs about "the way things are." When I was afraid that my first-ever online course hadn't gone well, why did I wait so long to reach out to anyone with my feelings of fear? Only in hindsight did I realize that it was because of the reasons that I just listed. I didn't want anyone to think that I was burden, a pity party of problems, or that I was a complete wreck all the time just because I was expressing that I felt like a wreck in this one area. I was afraid of opening up about my fears and hearing nothing in response, or of being told that I should have done it better. I was caught up in the image of having it all together—a classic Perfectionist fear routine.

My Story that I couldn't let go of the image of having it all together felt very real. I honestly didn't see that I was caught in it again until my friend pointed it out to me. In the same vein, a Martyr's fear routine might carry the Story that she'd be selfish to talk about her own difficulties, and that would feel very real. A person with a Pessimist fear routine might be convinced that there's no point in reaching out. Those with Saboteur fear routines are most likely to reach out, but then they'll sabotage the process of reaching out by choosing people who are unlikely to be supportive. Or, they might sabotage the process by reaching out, but subtly or overtly trying to get people to fix their problems for them.

Consider the fear routines that you identified earlier in this book. How might they be influencing the degree to which you reach out? Just as you did in the previous chapter, it's time to identify and then reframe those limiting Stories. Here are some examples:

I don't want to burden other people with my problems. → *My life's problems are not burdens and I deserve support.*

I feel weird and self-conscious when I get all bubbly and excited about something, so I usually make myself "calm down" before I'll share good news with other people. → *Sometimes, excitement can feel vulnerable because it's so real and authentic. I can show all sides of myself to others.*

They're just going to pity me. I hate it when other people pity me. → *I don't know whether anyone will pity me; that's their business. I can choose different support people if I sense that someone is pitying me.*

I'll feel stupid if they see just how messy my life is. → *I'm not stupid. I just feel vulnerable. Everyone's life is messy.*

They'll think that who I am when I'm upset, stressed, and reaching out, is who I am all the time. → *I can let them know that who I am when I'm upset isn't who I am all the time.*

I don't know if they'd accept me if I really told them the truth about who I am or how I feel. → *I have the power to move away from any relationships in which I'm not accepted for who I am. I can absolutely cultivate new relationships.*

They're going to see all the ways that I've screwed it up. → *If they see all the ways I screwed up, it might help bring me closer to this person.*

It's too embarrassing to open up and reveal more about myself, and then feel like there are crickets and they don't get it. I'm sure they wouldn't get it. → *I'm committed to being in relationship with a courageous community of people who truly "get it." We live in a world with billions of people, so someone, somewhere, will "get it."*

Write down the limiting Stories that you identified and start reframing them. Remember that you don't need to go wild with a reframe, unless it feels authentic to you to do that. Just take it one small step at a time in a positive direction.

Time to Reach Out

Now that you've walked through the process of applying the Courage Habit process to relationships with a practice person, it's time to directly practice the fourth part: reaching out. Where do you start?

Earlier, you identified a list of people who you felt embodied qualities of vulnerability, compassion, optimism, kindness, and empathy. These are the people who are "in your corner" so to speak when it comes to living with courage and going after what you truly desire. So, now you start by reaching out to those people. Instead of waiting for them to take the first step and offer you empathy or compassion, find some way to offer them these same gifts. Offer a friend empathy, optimism, compassion, confrontation with kindness, or a safe space for their vulnerability.

You could open this kind of dialogue simply by inviting them to share what's new, and listening. Or, you could let them know something you appreciate about them. Another option is a question that was first shared with me by Rich and Yvonne Dutra-St. John, cofounders of the award-winning Challenge Day organization: "If I really knew you, what would I know about you?"

If you've realized that your work is not about bolstering existing relationships, but rather more about creating new ones, decide to start practicing courageous connection with everyone you encounter. Take it on as a personal challenge. Ask the cashier how she's doing, and really make eye contact with her. When a coworker expresses frustration, validate how she feels.

Isolation is both a Story and a choice. You've got the tools to confront the Stories, and now you've got the tools to make connection your choice. Creating more connection in your life is, in my opinion, some of the most courageous work that we ever do.

Difficult Relationships

We've talked about relationships of convenience and courage-based relationships, but this chapter wouldn't be complete without also addressing difficult relationships. When I talk with clients about why they're hesitating to let themselves be fully seen by others as they make changes, they usually say something that resembles the following example: "My [husband, mother, father-in-law, boss, and so forth] would never support me. He'd [she'd] make sarcastic jokes about it. Any time I try to talk about [my big dream], he [she] tells me all the reasons why it won't work. He [she] brings up all the other people who have tried but failed. He [she] tells me to be realistic. I try to not let this person get to me, but after a while, I start feeling like he's [she's] right. How am I supposed to keep up the motivation to make this happen when I can't even get the people in my life on board?"

Most of my clients have found that as they stepped into being their most courageous selves that they also became a mirror for all the people in their lives. When we start making bold moves, other people inevitably start comparing themselves. "Why aren't I quitting the soul-sucking job to build the career I really want like she is? Why am I not writing the book that I know I have in me like she is? Why am I not volunteering for the cause that I truly believe in like she is?"

You might have watched someone in your life do something courageous and felt inspired to go after what you want. However, for others, watching you do something courageous might make them feel insecure, and their feelings of insecurity warrant some compassion. Your work is to keep that compassion in mind, while you make sure that you don't snuff your flame or give up on your dreams just so that they'll feel more comfortable. Even with difficult relationships, you can use the Courage Habit to navigate the bumps that arise, starting with unhooking from what other people think.

Unhooking from What Other People Think

The changes you make to step into a more courageous and authentic way of living and being will probably be met with a surprising mix of positive and negative responses from the people in your life. Sometimes the people you would most expect to be supportive will have the hardest time watching you change for the better. As a result, people making courageous changes in their lives have tried to hide or downplay their changes, which of course doesn't work. What we really want in life is a way to be true to who we are and still connect with others. What do you do when you want to make changes to your life and there's a possibility that those changes will trigger the criticism of others? Is the answer to just stop caring what anyone thinks?

Not really, I say. Most people who claim that they never care what anyone thinks of them are really working hard to *pretend* not to care. Deep down, they still care what people think, and the effort of pretending not to care becomes just as exhausting as the effort to pretend they are fearless.

I propose something different. Just like you don't want to get rid of fear, you don't want to get rid of the very natural human response of feeling hurt when someone is less than accepting of you. Instead, let's meet the hurt head-on, work through it, and adopt a mind-set that makes us less likely to get hooked into seeking someone's praise or approval.

Let's get real, though. Being who you really are and letting others see this new courageous self emerge is probably going to feel awkward or vulnerable at times. If your family of origin tends to be openly critical, it's hard to fully show up as yourself and be authentic, courageous, and real. That's why we'll be examining what I call "hiding out" behaviors that promote mistrust in relationships. Ultimately, you can't control what others think or say about the new direction that your life is going in, but you can make a conscious choice to stay aligned with the choices that you are making and practice behaviors that promote trust instead of hiding out from the truth of who you are.

Hiding Out

When it comes to hiding out and not letting your most coura-geous self be fully seen by others, everyone falls somewhere on the spectrum. On one end of the spectrum, people ultimately will claim the truth of who they are and how they want to live, but little bits of "hiding out" behaviors creep in. Perhaps they feel shy about sharing a success, have occasional worries about not being accepted fully, or go after a dream but not without hesitation—facing some big battles and resistance from themselves first. On the other end of the spectrum, "hiding out" behaviors might look like being condescending and dismissive of your own efforts when others ask what you're up to, living two different lives depending on who is noticing, and being completely unable to reach out when you're struggling.

Like so many other aspects of how we get through each day, "hiding out" behaviors can become such a default that we aren't always aware that we're engaging in them. Here are just a few examples of what hiding out can look like:

- You avoid reaching out during times of sadness or frustration. You feel embarrassed and vulnerable being seen during such times. You rationalize your avoidance by saying, "I don't want to bother other people," but really, you're hiding out.

- You notice yourself trying to fit in with whatever group you're with. You'll keep quiet on your opinions, and you assess how much you can reveal about your-self to others.

- You actively and intentionally try to hide specific things that are part of who you are that wouldn't be accepted by others, such as a creative longing, being in recovery from using a substance, your sexuality, or a marriage that is headed toward divorce.

- After spending time with someone, you worry about whether you said or did the right things.

- You'll do everything you can to avoid conflict in a relationship, including not being honest when something upsets you, because you don't trust that if you were honest the relationship could survive.

- You either don't touch a drop of alcohol to stay in control in front of others (one extreme) or you use alcohol or drugs to relax and can't really relax without them (the other extreme). In this case, the intention and Stories behind the use (or nonuse) is the issue.

- You don't trust that someone who is upset with you will just tell you about it and you'll work it out together. Someone being upset with you typically means that the friendship won't last.

- Because you feel self-conscious about telling the truth, your life as depicted on social media doesn't match your actual life. You appear happier and more contented in your social media updates than you actually are.

- People reach out to you to connect and you hesitate to reciprocate because you feel awkward.

In all the examples above, someone can be doing the work of the Courage Habit on an individual level, but if you're still hiding out from connection, there's a new playing ground for fears, such as not being enough. "Who I am isn't going to match people's expectations. So, to be good enough for them, I'll behave in the ways that they deem acceptable."

Pause for a moment. Access the body. Review the list of ways to hide out above and ask yourself: Which of these can I relate to?

In my experience of talking about this process with many people, the degree to which someone hides her most courageous self from the relationships in her life is directly related to how much and how often trust has been broken in relationships. Someone who has had an extreme experience of broken trust, such as abuse or being in a manipulative relationship, will be far more likely to hide her most courageous self and feel preoccupied with how she appears to other people.

This doesn't mean that it always takes an extreme experience of broken trust for someone to want to hide out. We hide who we really are or downplay the changes that we're making to maintain balance in relationships, to avoid criticism or being made fun of, or to be taken seriously (especially in the context of our work or in the workplace). We hide out because somewhere life has taught us that the responses of others can be painful, and that showing all of who you are comes with costs. You might know that you're *physically* safe around catty coworkers, but under the weight of their office gossip and undermining of you in meetings, you aren't *emotionally* safe. You might not ever be concerned that your mother-in-law is going to clock you with her purse as you walk by, but if you're acutely aware that at any moment she's going to make you the butt of a joke, you don't feel emotionally safe around her.

In our relationship with ourselves and others, we can practice behaviors that promote trust, or we can practice behaviors that create mistrust. The behaviors that create mistrust will emerge as a kind of dance that looks like this:

1. When we have trouble trusting in ourselves or in others, we have trouble feeling safe, so we hide out.

2. Because of the hiding out, it becomes harder to trust in ourselves or for others to trust us.

3. As it becomes harder to trust ourselves or for others to trust us, we're likely to turn to more hiding out.

It continues to spiral from there. For example, your boss doesn't trust you, so she micromanages you, which causes you to resent and mistrust her ability to be a great boss. As each person looks to the other person to be the first one to change and be more trustworthy, both parties stay locked in opposition, and it only ever becomes harder to trust as each person waits for the other to take the high ground. If you've ever participated in this dance, you know that sometimes trust can become so damaged between two people that even when you offer an olive branch the person still thinks that you're just fooling them.

So, how can we stop this dance? Since we can't control other people or their reactions, we change the dynamic by looking at any Stories that we're believing that might prompt us to hide out. We then reframe those Stories and replace the hiding out with reaching out. Again, you can't control other people or their reactions, which means you can't control whether they'll be happy about the changes you're making. What you can control is the impulse to edit yourself in order to make others more comfortable.

Consider how you pretend, shift, change, or alter your behavior around certain people in your life. How do you edit yourself around critical people? People who are unsupportive? People who are typically negative? Changing our behavior, holding ourselves back, and making decisions based on what other people think often make up the last wall that needs to come tumbling down as we make the transition from being stuck in a fear routine to living our most courageous life. Our fear routines and Inner Critic drive the Stories that someone else's criticism will feel too awful to bear, that we'll be left by the people that we love if we tell the truth, or that our marriages can't withstand the difficult but necessary conversations.

"Hiding Out" Stories

Take some time to consider the following prompts to uncover any Stories that might influence your "hiding out" behaviors. I call these your "hiding out" stories. Write down the questions and your responses on a sheet of paper or on the worksheet available at http://www.yourcourageouslife.com/courage-habit, if you're so inclined.

1. Ask yourself the following question, three times. Each time that you ask it, pause and take a deep breath. After you've asked it three times, begin writing. Make sure that you don't censor yourself, even if what you write doesn't initially seem to make sense. If at any point you feel stumped for an answer, stop and close your eyes, pausing to ask yourself the question again. Here's the question: Where in my life do I "hide out"?

2. Finish the following sentence: I can't be myself around _____ because…

3. Finish the following sentence: I don't know if I could handle it if _____ happened, because...

4. Finish the following sentence: People wouldn't like me if they knew _____ about me, because...

5. Finish the following sentence: I wouldn't want anyone to know about _____ [money problems, a deep desire to change careers, sexual longings, a huge mistake I made, a choice that's controversial]...

6. Finish the following sentence: I'm most likely to pretend to be someone I'm not when _____ because...

After writing your responses to these questions, it's time to distill them down to specific, clear sentences in order to break down the Stories that underlie them. For example, if for question 2 you wrote many different reasons why you can't be yourself, try simplifying the sentence into the following: "My Story is that I can't be myself when things are difficult." Or, if for question 5 you wrote something like "I wouldn't want anyone to know the amount of the debt we're in," you could re-write the sentence into "My Story is that I can't be myself if my family is in a bunch of debt." You're asked to put sentences into an authoritative "I" form because working on your own Story about what other people's judgments are of you will do more for you than trying to change someone else's opinion.

After you've rewritten these statements in the "I can't be myself..." structure above, you'll literally have a list in front of you of the Stories that underlie any impulses to hide out, rather than reach out. Access your body. How does it feel to review this list? Which Stories seem to jump off the page and "get you in the gut" with how true they feel?

The last step in this process is to start questioning each sentence as a possible Story and reframe any Stories that are accurate for you. Remember your tools of reframing from the last chapter, and that you're not being asked to put a sparkly overcoat on a difficult or painful situation. Rather, reframing your Stories involves acknowledging where you are, and stretching in a more positive direction. Here are a few examples:

> *I can't be myself around people who are judgmental. →*
> *I can notice where I feel an impulse to hide out around*
> *people who are judgmental. → I can question how much*
> *power I want to give to a judgmental statement. → I can*
> *choose to ignore someone's judgment. → I can respond*
> *to someone's judgment by asking them to rephrase their*
> *statement, respectfully.*

> *I can't be myself if I'm in a bunch of debt. → I can better*
> *understand where I've tied money to my identity. → I can*
> *question who I would be without the debt, and see how*
> *to be more of that now. → I can redefine living happily,*
> *even with debt. → I can start letting people know that I'm*
> *in debt, but I'm committed to getting out of it. → I can*
> *choose not to be ashamed of having debt. → I can take*
> *pride in the fact that I'm working on my debt problem.*

Whether we trust in our ability to withstand criticism, or whether we hide out to desperately avoid it, is always based on our capital-S Stories. How much you trust yourself and your ability to navigate the responses of others has everything to do with how much power you give to the Stories. You deserve to feel full ownership over your life and your choices, and to feel free to be totally and completely who you truly are without fear of what others will do or say.

Rehabilitating Relationships

I said earlier that to stop hiding out, we need to identify, question, and reframe the Stories that might prompt us to hide out, and then start practicing "reaching out" behaviors. So, let's not keep this task of working out difficult relationships theoretical. You don't need to wait until the next time that you are talking to someone who judges you before you can apply this work.

You've been thinking of a practice person as you've been working through the exercises in this chapter. Complete any piece of an exercise that you haven't finished. Silently think of the person and access the body in some way. Then, listen to what the Critic has to say about the person, or about your interaction with the person. Then, note the Stories that arise, and immediately begin the process of reframing them. Last, identify a "reaching out" behavior that you could practice with this person. For example:

Practice Vulnerability: Be honest about who you are when you interact with this person, and intentionally choose that authenticity in your words and actions.

Optimism: Decide that you'll remain optimistic about the potential for this relationship to change.

Empathy: Promise yourself not to offer the person advice.

Compassion: Where could you offer this person compassion?

Confrontation with Kindness: If you've been resisting putting a boundary in place, and this person launches into criticism, consider confronting him or her with kindness in the form of the simple statement "I notice that this doesn't feel good." Or, give yourself some kindness: Is it time for you to stop resisting offering vulnerability, compassion, optimism, or empathy to this person?

Practice your "reaching out" behaviors with this person from a place of deep commitment to honor the value of courage in your life, and not from a place of wanting this person to be different or wanting a result. In earlier chapters, you practiced listening to the Inner Critic without attachment. The idea is that regardless of what the Critic says to you, you don't take it as truth. If you're trying to improve an existing connection in your life, especially one that has historically been difficult, the tool is essentially the same. Here's an example: A family member asks you what you've been up to lately, and instead of hiding out by downplaying the truth with saying, "Oh, things are fine, busy as usual," you decide to be fully seen. You say, "I'm considering a career change. I'm really ready to leave my old job, and I think I'm getting some-where in finding out what's next for me."

The family member first responds with, "It's a terrible economy right now for a career change." Then, she moves into full-on criticism. "After all that money you spent on your MBA, I can't believe you'd do something so foolish as to completely change careers." If this family member was the Inner Critic, you'd say "Re-do, please," because your Inner Critic is part of you, and you get to call the shots when it comes to your own headspace. But, in real life, you can't *make* people rephrase something or change their behavior. When it comes to friends or family members who are unsupportive, negative, or critical, there are two options. First, you can try and speak about how you feel and directly request that the two of you identify and practice more "reaching out" behaviors. Or, you accept that the person is going to behave how they behave and set up appropriate boundaries to care for yourself, protecting yourself from the impact of their negativity.

When Janelle began talking to her husband about how overwhelmed she felt and making requests for his help, he initially felt so overwhelmed by the thought of taking on more that he wasn't open to hearing it—period. At first, Janelle had to stop herself from handling something for him, just as she had to stop herself from handling things for her children, so that he would see that she had a real boundary around creating more space for herself. That was enough to bring him to the table for a conversation in which they could both talk about dividing responsibilities more equitably.

Carolyn, by contrast, had almost no relationship with her father and much of her work was in reaching out to see if he wanted more contact. After several attempts, he didn't respond, which initially caused Carolyn deep pain. After spending some time working through her feelings about her father and grieving the relationship that never was, Carolyn reframed an old Story that her life had somehow been less because he was absent. She realized that she couldn't really know if her life had been harder without him, and given his behavior after she tried to reach out, perhaps she truly had been better off. These are just two examples of how people can take on this work around connection.

Whenever you think a relationship can be improved, the Courage Habit process can be utilized. Access the body so that you can take deep breaths and stay grounded during a difficult conversation. Listen without attachment to what the other person says. For instance, if the individual doesn't agree with you or doesn't want to do things your way, it's best to listen without attachment. Understand that just as Critics might put down your ideas due to their own insecurity, people who love us very much can be just as limited when it comes to their own fears and insecurities. Sometimes, people criticize us because they are afraid for us. Just as you work with the Critic, rather than avoiding, pleasing, or attacking, you can work with people who are willing to create more respectful communication. Reframe limiting Stories about yourself, or about how much connection is possible. You can even build reframing into how you respond to someone who isn't supportive. Here are just a few examples:

> I'm hearing you share a lot about what could go wrong, and I've thought of those things, too. I'm really excited about this decision and would prefer to talk about all of the things that could go right.

> When you tell me that I seem different, there's a tone there that I'm interpreting as maybe being critical. Is it? I feel good about the changes I'm making, and I'd like to request your support.

> I want to respect your opinion, and now I've heard it— really and truly. I've listened. I still think that the choices I'm making are the choices that are best for me.

Last, continually strive to reach out rather than hide out. Let go of image, and be willing to be vulnerable. Offer empathy, before you offer advice. In other words? Treat people how you'd want to be treated. When people aren't willing to respect the changes that you're making in your life, you might need to make some difficult yet courageous choices. These choices could include:

> You might limit what you talk about with them, so long as it doesn't mean editing who you are.

You might limit your contact with them, either in frequency or limit it to a certain form of communication, such as email or phone rather than in-person visits.

You might be around them, yet continue to relentlessly speak about the need for respectful communication.

You might need to respectfully state that right now it's not feeling like a good time to continue communication, but that you're open to communicating later if the communication is respectful.

You might need to respectfully state that you are choosing to exit the relationship.

You could decide that no matter what someone throws your way, you're going to view them with love and compassion.

When my clients are wrestling with these decisions, they often ask me, "How do I know what choice to make?" I can't give them an answer for that, but I do suggest that before they exit a relationship, they fully clean up their side of the street. Change can start with these simple lines: "Hey, things aren't feeling good. Can we talk about it?"

If you're ready to start feeling more connected to the people around you and to start meeting people who are on the same journey to more courageous living, start applying the four parts of the Courage Habit to your relationships. Access your body, and be honest about what you feel. Notice your Inner Critic and your criticisms of others, and listen without attachment. Clarify your limiting capital-S Stories—about them and yourself—and reframe them. And, finally, take action to reach out and create a wider community through practicing behaviors that reflect the value of courage.

Creating the Ripple Effect

Navigating difficult conversations isn't the only arena for applying the Courage Habit process. Janelle, the mother of three we talked about in earlier chapters, called in with some interesting news. "Kate, have you ever applied these steps to parenting? I've got my kids using them!" She went on to explain that during one particularly frustrating day when she was negotiating a three-way argument between her two oldest children, she had stopped and closed her eyes to access the body, and one of her children had asked her what she was doing.

"I'm accessing the body," she told him. "It's what I do when I'm feeling tense and need to relax."

"I want to try it," he said.

What unfolded next completely surprised Janelle. She explained to the kids that the next time there was an argument, everyone needed to stop and access the body and then listen to what the other person was saying. Then, if someone was saying something unkind, something that was leading them to feel frustrated or sad or that felt hurtful, they could ask each other to use the tool of "Re-do, Please."

When Janelle's son asked what to do if the other person was still being mean, Janelle got stuck for a moment, but then she knew exactly how to explain the idea of reframing limiting Stories to her son. "Sometimes people get angry or act mean, but we can work it out. It doesn't mean that we don't love them, or that they aren't still our friends." Then, she told me, she had added the tool of reaching out by reminding him that he could always play with someone else, or come to her if he wanted to talk things through.

People I've worked with have also used different parts of the Courage Habit as an underpinning to improving communication in their marriages, and not just during times of conflict. Taylor, newly married to her husband, Ben, once shared that he had been incredibly curious about the work she was doing in coaching. She told him about the four parts of the Courage Habit, and they started talking about them over dinner each night. They decided to start each meal by breathing and truly getting present with one another. Ben tended to withdraw when he was stressed about work, so they made a pact that Ben would make a point of reaching out on hard days by letting Taylor know what was on his mind. And, Taylor would make a point of reaching out by listening with empathy rather than offering advice. (Ben particularly loathed receiving advice.) When Ben could trust that he would truly be heard, he opened up more and he and Taylor felt closer to one another.

There's a ripple effect that happens when even one individual decides to start practicing the Courage Habit process. The first three parts help you to do the inner work, and reaching out is the step that brings living a courageous life full-circle. The best part is that there is no need to work to "convert" anyone. You can model how to honor the values of courage and be willing to let your most courageous self be visible, and other people just become interested in what you've got going on that has you happier and more fully alive. They, too, want to stop being limited by fear or self-doubt and will get curious about the process.

While the issues that my clients (mostly women) bring to coaching are deeply personal, they are also rooted in collective problems faced by our society. Janelle was overwhelmed as a mother in part because of the expectations our society places on women to be endlessly self-sacrificing without giving much in the way of childcare, financial support, or emotional resources to women who become mothers. Carolyn, who lost a parent and was plunged into extreme debt through no fault of her own, was like many people in our society who have no safety net available and who become extremely vulnerable when the worst happens. Taking these facts into account, it might seem as if individual work is only ever a Band-Aid for a much larger problem that needs to be addressed.

However, I'd also argue that this perspective doesn't consider the necessity of doing individual work so that you can expand your resilience to do collective work. We also need tools to work through our own personal fears about wide-scale change. We may look around and see the things that we deeply desire to change in the world, yet the Critic is still stuck in a Pessimist routine, saying, "The problem is too big; be realistic. It's not like you can do anything about it." It's only through becoming individuals who practice courage that we'll create a world where everyone is willing to face fear by asking the hard questions and taking action even when there's self-doubt.

Moving Forward

At this point, you've covered an incredible amount of ground! In this chapter alone you put the final Courage Habit step into place by thinking about how you can integrate your Primary Focus and desires for change into the rest of your life. I really hope that you'll consider taking just one more active step as part of the work to reach out and create community. Please consider joining the Courage Habit online community, which is a pretty incredible group of people who are committed to practicing the four parts of the Courage Habit. Head to http://www.yourcourageouslife.com /courage-habit for information about how to join the group.

After joining, feel free to introduce yourself and let us know what part of the book you're currently working through and what you're noticing. There is an entire world of people out there who deeply desire courageous connection. If you've read this far, I think you're one of us. You can also share any places where you might feel stuck. (We're happy to help!) If you share something you're proud of, we're excited to cheer you on and get yet another reminder that big, bold things are in fact possible, and you are the proof.

There is one last piece to this process that mirrors how I work in a coaching relationship: taking time to review and reflect on the work you've done and declare completion on this leg of the process. In the next chapter, you'll have an opportunity to identify any last spaces where you're holding yourself back. I'll also be encouraging you to truly get grounded in feeling proud of all that you've done. Take a breath, and let's do a little truth-telling about just how amazing you are and how far you've come.

Chapter 7

Reflecting On Your Courageous Life

This entire journey started because on a rainy, gloomy winter day in San Francisco, I woke up feeling lackluster, and had felt this way for far too many days in a row. I decided to pay attention to that and ask myself what had led me there and what I could do to change. Looking honestly at why I was unhappy in my career became the catalyst for something much bigger: getting honest about the fear-based choices that I had made, understanding and releasing my own self-imposed limits, and letting my most courageous self emerge.

Going through this process and regularly returning to the process as new challenges and fears arise enables me to support others who are working the Courage Habit steps. In the coaching world, we treat exhaustion, unhappiness, and other body-based signals as being worth listening to. We look at the fear routines that derail us whenever we aren't conscious of the role they play. We keep orienting toward a bigger vision by determining a Primary Focus, talking about who that most courageous self is, and then creating room for that bolder self to emerge. Then, the work begins of taking action toward that change and practicing the four steps of the Courage Habit. Ultimately, this work is never just about a goal or "achieving" the Primary Focus. Deciding on a focus for change is just the doorway to doing things differently, dreaming big, getting creative, and stepping forward to take emotional risks in the name of creating the life that you want.

The best thing about the Courage Habit tools is that they lead you beyond goals and into a more courageous way of being. They're the steps that you take to live a more courageous, more vitally alive life. I've watched in awe as people have done things that they had never thought they'd be capable of, all in the name of their own happiness. People have found their voices and stood up to domineering relatives, totally altering the course of old, entrenched patterns in their family. They've confronted addictions, given up everything, and traveled the world. They've walked away from lucrative careers to do things with their lives that might have appeared ordinary to the outside world, but that were extraordinary for their own souls.

What's more, I've seen these tools go beyond a person's individual goals. Clients have applied the Courage Habit to parenting, social justice work and activism, cooperative education, non-profits, creativity and the arts, and shifting the dynamics within a corporation. These are pragmatic tools that you can learn, share, and use with others. If enough of us are practicing them, the result could be pretty amazing. We could see a world where more people are practicing courage, deciding that it's worth it to face fears and find solutions to our collective challenges.

In this chapter, I'll be inviting you to reflect on your process and complete an assessment and review designed to help you feel truly proud of what you've invested. Before we do that, it's important that I offer support around one last piece of the puzzle—the "it's still not enough" Story that can keep you from seeing how far you've truly come.

Growth as a Process

You're going to find that even after doing this work, life's loose ends, challenges, and stuck spaces will still crop up. For example, maybe you've come to realize just how important a Primary Focus goal is, but even with regular effort, you're still not quite there. This can arouse feelings of disappointment, incite a Critic that uses this as irrefutable "evidence" for why things can't change, and make it more difficult to release those *This is impossible* Stories that you've been trying to reframe.

Does this mean that the process didn't work? What do you do with the fact that even with progress, there are still things in life that feel stuck? What you do is commit to trusting the process of change by returning to the four parts of the Courage Habit. Access the body, and note what you feel. Listen without attachment to the Critic and the Stories it brings, such as *Things are supposed to be farther along than this* or *Things still feel stuck in my life and they shouldn't*. Reach out to others who will remind you that even if life has challenges, there's still a lot of good, and that what you've invested in your journey has been worth it.

Trusting the process will mean that you give yourself some room to be an imperfect person, living an imperfect life (as we all are), and recognizing that the power to be happy is your own. You can still be happy even if you didn't do it all perfectly, if you still have things you'd like to change, and if your progress isn't as far along as you might have hoped it would be by now. We get so much conditioning from the media and Hollywood portraying a "happy life" as one in which things are neatly wrapped up that we don't even always know what an authentically happy life looks like.

An authentically happy life is one that contains moments that are messy, unfinished, and sometimes stuck. It also contains beautiful moments where you follow your soul's calling and decide that you won't stand for another minute of the status quo, and you may even see your dreams realized! A happy, courageous life isn't an either-or equation. What's messy, unfinished, or stuck is a reflection of the growth process that we're in, and it will be ongoing.

Just as we've got to unhook from the lie of "forever fearlessness," we've got to unhook from the lie that growth only happens when you've achieved an outcome (and thus, have a "perfect" life). Growth must be put in its proper context: It's a long-game proposition, and sometimes you'll grow more and at other times less. I can promise you that all the people profiled in this book live better lives than they were living before they started to go after their Primary Focus goals or practice the steps of the Courage Habit. However, none of them live perfect lives in which they don't ever encounter struggles.

In the years since I shifted things in my own life, I've felt lucky beyond belief to have created a life that feels like *me*. At the same time, challenges have still come up. I've been diagnosed with an autoimmune disease, hit financial challenges that seemed insurmountable at the time, grieved lost friendships, and more.

Again and again, I have turned to the process of the Courage Habit to see myself through. Right alongside the difficulties I've experienced, and because I've remained committed to the Courage Habit steps, I've also transcended those difficult circumstances and created a lot of good! I married a man who is also my best friend, became the CEO of my own company, gave birth to our daughter after doctors gave me a pretty grim infertility diagnosis and all fertility treatments had failed, met women who are not just friends but my soul sisters, contributed my work to national news media, and stepped into financial security and sovereignty over my time that seemed impossible before I began using the Courage Habit tools. That's an example of the long game: The challenges still arise, but in facing difficulties with the Courage Habit process, you can continue to be able to live from the place of your most courageous self.

Trusting the process and putting growth in context is one of the "secrets" to living a happier life. Clarifying and then unhooking from your own Stories about where you "should" be, and allowing yourself to be where you are and trust the process you're in, takes you out of the exhausting struggle to be better. Instead, you get the relief of being just where you are, and being proud of what you've done.

If you think that there might be any Stories of *I should be farther along*, or *Since I still feel stuck around* _____ , *it means I haven't truly become more courageous*, take some time to untangle those Stories, now. Write them down on a piece of paper, use the same process that you used in Chapter 5 to question those Stories, and then reframe them in the direction of trusting your process.

If you're having trouble questioning and reframing those Stories, just think back to the way things felt when you first started this journey, reading the first pages of this book. How were you handling fear then? Were you trying to ignore it or push it away? What place did your deepest dreams hold in your life? Did you feel like they had free rein to emerge?

What has shifted since then? Notice that I didn't ask what was perfect, whether you've got your life completely in order, or if your Primary Focus has been "achieved." It's great if these things have happened, but noticing what has shifted and being present to the ways in which you are growing and changing is enough. In fact, it's the most important thing. That's how you honor the value of courage and live your courageous life.

Even after all these years of practice, every time I stretch into some new space, I know that I will again feel some level of fear or self-doubt. I don't see it as a failing that I still feel those things. Instead, I remember that those cues of fear won't go away, because that's not how life works. Instead, I can examine my routines. I can also take fear and self-doubt as a sign that something deeply matters to me. Instead of responding to the fear in the old, habitual ways, I get curious, and the fear sometimes even turns to excitement! I know that if I'm willing to be in process with each part of the Courage Habit, I'm going to find my way to something great. Life can get even better than it already is. There's so much more that awaits you as you work with these tools.

Reflection and Review

Before we close out our time together, let's reflect on and review your process. As you answer each question, access the body by finding that place within you that's willing to celebrate what you've done. See if you can connect to that little buzz of excitement that is felt in the body when you're proud of yourself. If your Critic pops up to tell you that you haven't done enough to deserve celebration, use "Re-do, Please" and do a bit of reframing for any Stories that the Critic offers. Then get back to celebrating, and push yourself to find those true, full-tilt celebration sensations in your body.

If your work with this book was to mirror a cue-routine-reward loop, this celebration would be the ultimate reward! You get to celebrate the work that you've invested in your process. *Whatever work you've done is enough!* Deciding that you'll believe the Story that you've done *enough* in this read of *The Courage Habit* is part of supporting your most courageous self. Give yourself credit for what you have done, instead of telling the Story that you should have done more.

Some people will love answering these questions with their favorite journal or on the worksheet available at http://www.your courageouslife.com/courage-habit. Others will want to do this exercise in a different way. You could try walking and pausing to answer a question as you walk; or speaking the question aloud, slowly; or getting visual—paint, make a collage, doodle your responses.

1. How was I handling fear at the start of this journey? Was I avoiding my Critic, pleasing it, or attacking it?

2. What was my specific fear routine? What were some things I noticed myself doing, saying, thinking, or believing as a result? What cue-routine-reward loops was I locked into?

3. What were the three Primary Focus goals that I chose for this process?

4. Describe your most courageous self and the day-to-day life that she wants to live.

5. How have you chosen to practice regularly accessing the body? Write it down, and then write down how consistent you are at practicing it. Are there any adjustments you want to make to your practice, such as becoming more consistent? Are there additional

ways of accessing the body you want to experiment with?

6. How has accessing the body been helpful? Note some specific insights you've arrived at. Maybe there were times when accessing the body reduced stress or was particularly helpful at stopping a habitual fear routine before it had time to start.

7. How did you handle the Critic prior to starting this work? Did you tend to avoid it, push it away, or fight against it?

8. What are some changes you've made in your relationship with the Critic? For instance, do you listen to it without attachment, at least some of the time? Do you view it with more compassion, seeing that it's coming from a wounded place?

9. What are some specific things the Critic says that you'd still like to work on? Write them down exactly as the Critic says them. Take a breath with each statement as you write. You don't need to work through these statements now, unless you want to use "Re-do, Please." You can just celebrate the fact that you notice the Critic, and that you're willing to do the ongoing work of shifting the Critic's voice.

10. What are some limiting Stories that you've worked through during this process? Write down what they were and write down your reframes.

11. How often were you reaching out prior to starting this work? How often are you practicing "reaching

out" behaviors now? Who are you practicing with (strangers, a family member, your children, coworkers, and so forth)?

12. How has your Primary Focus shifted or changed through this process? (It might not have shifted; this is just an opportunity to notice if it has.)

13. How has your most courageous self shifted or changed through this process? Note any additional insights or realizations, a deepening of what you want, or any places where you completely changed directions. These shifts are positive. They indicate that you're present to your process!

14. In addition to the benefits that honoring the value of courage will bring to your own life, what benefits are brought to others' lives because you've done this work? (In other words, what's the ripple effect that benefits your family, community, workplace, or the wider world?)

After completing these questions, do something that honors the process you've undertaken. You could share about your process, share these questions with someone else who is completing the Courage Habit, or give the questions an honoring space somewhere. Fold the paper containing your answers and tuck it under your pillow, plant the paper in the earth, or put it on your home altar if you have one. I personally love to put my responses to these questions in an envelope, write the date on the envelope, and then set it aside. A year later, a reminder in my calendar prompts me to open the envelope and connect to my gratitude for having put the work in, as well as to see how far I've come.

Where We Go from Here

When I'm working with a coaching client who is ready to discontinue coaching sessions, we declare completion of this part of our coaching relationship. We both understand that the client will always have more ways that she wants to grow, but that the process she underwent has a beginning, a middle, and an end, and now she's got some tools for continuing her growth process herself. Before we part ways, I always ask people to think about what they want to create now from this new vantage point. What beckons on the horizon? What new adventure awaits? That's what I'll be asking you to do as we close out this part of the Courage Habit process.

First, let's start with a declaration and summary of what has shifted, keeping it simple. I offer some sample sentences below. Choose one thing that has shifted and write it down in the journal you've been keeping during the Courage Habit process.

I was someone who felt stuck in believing _____, and now I realize _____.

I've moved from feeling _____, to feeling _____.

I needed help with _____, and I'm proud that I've taken action steps toward _____.

I was struggling with _____, and now I'm more able to _____.

I used to be more afraid of _____, and now I'm courageous enough to _____.

What would you like to create from this new vantage point? You're a person who has undertaken a journey of self-inquiry, being willing to keep asking the tough questions even if you encountered fear along the way. Ask yourself: What's next? What's your ongoing personal work? Consider the next twelve weeks of your life. If you were beginning this process anew, starting at this vantage point after you've learned so much more about yourself and what you're capable of, what would you want to create? Sometimes, clients answer that they'd just like to keep refining the Primary Focus that they had already set out to create, in which case their "new" Primary Focus goals would be "Continue my work with _____." Other times, clients share that they've got a new vision on the horizon, and they're excited to roll up their sleeves and see what else is going to unfold. It's completely up to you.

If there's something that immediately comes to mind, write that down, and you know the rest! Otherwise, turn to the work you did for Chapter 1 to clarify your most courageous self. At the end of that chapter, you articulated a Primary Focus with three specific items. Inevitably, there's something that didn't make it onto that list of three things, and perhaps now is the time for you to take it on. Or, try going through each of the exercises for clarifying your most courageous self again, bringing a beginner's mind to the process.

Another way to build this work into your life is to make it seasonal. Every year before the New Year, my husband and I have a date night where we ask ourselves what we want to be, do, or have during the year to come. We write down our desires for the year and share them with one another, and check in with each other periodically throughout the year. I write down action steps related to what I want to create for the year in my calendar, and those become prompts to keep checking in with myself. In recent years, I've invited everyone online to participate. I sent newsletter subscribers the free annual "Courageous Living Planner," a down-loadable planner that has Courage Habit tools tied to monthly and quarterly prompts.

Whichever path you choose, take time now to write down your three new Primary Focus goals. Honoring the value of courage and responding differently to old fear routines is ongoing work, but understand that now you are very much equipped with the tools for doing this on your own. You've got this!

Of course, this never has to be a solitary process. I hope that you'll join us in our free Courage Habit community on Facebook. Head to http://www.yourcourageouslife.com/courage-habit to get started. Any time you want to connect with other Courage Habit participants from around the world, you can find each other using the #couragehabit hashtag on social media. You can also tag me on Instagram (@katecourageous) or head to Facebook.com/Your CourageousLife; I'll be excited to give you a congratulatory shout-out. Let all of us celebrate with you as you complete each part of the process!

Thank you so much for being part of this book—and truly, you are *part* of the writing of this book. I'm so incredibly honored to have been part of your personal process in this small way. Every single word was written while thinking of people like you, who will use these tools to create a better life for yourself and the people in your world. I offer a deep, deep bow.

Acknowledgments

I'm devoted to the written word, but when it comes to both love and gratitude, these are the times when words feel inadequate. The fourth part of the Courage Habit process is to reach out and create community, and truly, if I hadn't been practicing that step regularly, I'd never be here.

First and foremost, so much gratitude goes to the clients I've worked with, the readers who visit YourCourageousLife.com, and the thousands of people I've interacted with through attending online seminars, taking courses, showing up for workshops, and conferences, listening to podcasts, and participating in programs. I see you, I hear you, and I'm with you, both in the moments of your (totally normal!) fear and in the moments when you choose to practice courage. Really-really, truly-truly. This book is for you and I'm holding you in my heart.

I met Kimber Simpkins, author of *Full*, at a birthday party. I told her that I was working on the courage to send out my book proposal. Kimber told me she'd loved working with the team at New Harbinger Publications, and she shared the name of a contact person so that I could send in my proposal. Quite literally, Kimber, your generosity and openheartedness have forever changed my life.

Kimber wasn't kidding when she said that the team at New Harbinger is amazing. Camille Hayes, thank you for seeing something in my proposal and for the privilege of this experience, which I'll never forget. Vicraj Gill, your perceptiveness and the love and care with which you edit a writer's work has made me a better writer. This book wouldn't be what it is without your guidance—thank you. To Julie Bennett and the marketing team, thank you for your warm reception and an immediate sense of inclusiveness. To everyone at New Harbinger: I know that y'all do this every day, but...*Holy smokes! We did it—we created a book!*

Bari Tessler, author of *The Art of Money*, has not only taught me about practicing courage when it comes to my finances, she also wrote the foreword to this book. There isn't enough chocolate in the world to convey my thanks. (But hey, Bari, you know that I'll try.)

I've had the honor of meeting some incredible people who have offered friendship, or offered support and supersavvy business wisdom, or who have helped me change my life for the better. I'm gobsmacked to have met them, and I strongly suggest that you Google all of them, stat. They include Kira Sabin, Laura Simms, Rachel W. Cole, Tiffany Han, Andrea Owen, Laurie Wagner, Amy E. Smith, Vivienne McMaster, Dr. Brené Brown, Marianne Elliott, Tara Sophia Mohr, Dyana Valentine, Cheri Huber, Jenn Lee, Michelle Ward, Nisha Moodley, Margo Brockman, Allison Tyler, Christine Mason-Miller, Kelly Rae Roberts, Lianne Raymond, Tara Gentile, McCabe Russell, Tanya Geisler, Julie Daley, Andrea Scher, and Stacy DeLaRosa.

Molly Mahar of Stratejoy, thank you for those times when you've hopped on the phone with me to explain how things work. Theresa Reed's tarot readings are on freaking point. My lawyer,

Robert Kelly, deserves a shout-out for rocking the contracts. After I became a mother, Holly Wick, owner of Athletic Soles in Petaluma, helped me to reconnect with myself through the sport of triathlon, and in a funny sort of way, that was the impetus for me to get back to taking my writing seriously. And, speaking of writing, thank you to the graduate English program at UC Davis. Thank you to Dr. Robert Archambeau of Lake Forest College, who encouraged my writing, and thank you to Dr. David Boden, who first got me interested in studying how people tick.

Adrianne Laconi is my company's badass operations manager, and she keeps me grounded in more ways than she knows. My company couldn't have operated without her these past few years. And, a big thanks to the leadership team of the Courageous Living Coach Certification, which has included such powerful women as Valerie Tookes, Lara Heacock, Liz Applegate, Paula Jenkins, Michelle Crank, and Julie Houghton. Molly K. Larkin, and Natalia Chouklina also sat with me for a spell. I know that we call it a life coach training program, but, of course, let's just be real: we're courage junkies. We make no apologies for the fact that we just can't get enough. #TribeCLCC for the win!

Carl Rogers is my homeboy and Pema Chödrön is my guru. Carl has passed and I've never met Pema, but I feel that my life wouldn't shine as brightly if I hadn't been exposed to their work. Irvin Yalom, your books have helped me to understand myself and my clients better. Charles Duhigg, your writing on habit-formation made the work accessible for me and, among other things, revolutionized how we put our toddler to bed. For that, any time you're in town, dinner is on me! The spirit of Bob Rado is behind the words, too, and I send a deep bow to my energetic lineage and my family on the other side. And, of course, to my family that's alive and well: thank you. A shout-out to my sister, Vanessa Swoboda, for her encouragement when I hit a fork in the road.

Rich and Yvonne Dutra-St. John of the Challenge Day organization have taught me about the power of making a different choice in an instant and how life changing that can be, as well as creating "love that leaves God speechless."

Danielle LaPorte, thank you for helping me to finally make the connection that I can write my own damned permission slip—*thank you very much*. And, deep gratitude for being willing to say, "Well, fuck that diagnosis," at a time when everyone else was offering pithy advice. Thank you for your life-changing brand of generosity.

Valerie Tookes, we've been friends for more than a decade, and when I think of the most courageous people I know, you are always at the top of the list. I see how big and wide you love, and how you step out into the arena over and over again even if you're shaking, because love and living fully alive are worth it. Don't think for a second that the rest of us are fooled, because behind the introverted exterior you are a *force*. Thank you for being my sister.

Matthew Marzel started out as our couples coach, then he became my personal coach, was the officiant who married my husband and me, and was there the day my daughter was born. Across years of sessions, he's seen me at my angriest, saddest, most devastated, and most confused. He never believed that those states were who I truly was at my core, which is precisely why and how I've been able to transcend any of the painful stuff.

To Anika, my daughter: Before you were born, an interviewer asked what my hopes and dreams for you were. I said that I didn't care whether you went to college or ever "achieved" anything. All I really want is for you to live a life in which you can completely trust yourself and trust in your own inherent goodness. You are only three years old right now, so feel free to show this to me later if I ever change my mind on the college part.

To my husband, Andy Rado, you are my always. You've supported absolutely every risk I've wanted to take. You're my best friend, a total hottie, an incredible father, and the only person I want to snuggle up next to at the end of a day. People say, "I couldn't have done it without you," and in our case, truer words were never spoken. I choose you, and me, and us, all day every day.

Bibliography

Ashby, F. G., B. O. Turner, and J. C. Horvitz. 2010. "Cortical and Basal Ganglia Contributions to Habit Learning and Automaticity." *Trends in Cognitive Sciences* 14(5): 208–215. Retrieved from https://labs.psych.ucsb.edu/ashby/gregory /reprints/sdarticle.pdf.

Blackledge, J. T. 2015. "Comparing ACT and CBT: Defusion vs. Restructuring." March 10. https://www.newharbinger.com /blog/comparing-act-and-cbt-defusion-vs -restructuring.

Brown, B. 2015. *Daring Greatly: How the Courage to Be Vulnerable Transforms the Way We Live, Love, Parent, and Lead.* London: Penguin.

Chödrön, P. 1997. *When Things Fall Apart: Heart Advice for Difficult Times.* Boulder, CO: Shambhala Publications.

Christou-Champi, S., T. F. D. Farrow, and T. L. Webb. 2015. "Automatic Control of Negative Emotions: Evidence That Structured Practice Increases the Efficiency of Emotion Regulation." *Cognition and Emotion* 29(2): 319–331.

Crocker, J., M. A. Olivier, and N. Nuer. 2009. "Self-Image Goals and Compassionate Goals: Costs and Benefits." *Self Identity* 8(2–3): 251–269. Retrieved from https://www.ncbi.nlm.nih .gov/pmc/articles/PMC3017354.

Duhigg, C. 2014. *The Power of Habit: Why We Do What We Do in Life and Business.* New York: Random House.

Dutra-St. John, Y., and R. Dutra-St. John. 2009. *Be the Hero You've Been Waiting For.* Walnut Creek, CA: Challenge Associates.

Dzierzak, L. 2008. "Factoring Fear: What Scares Us and Why." *Scientific American.* Retrieved from https://www.scientific american.com/article/factoring-fear-what-scares.

Goldin, P. R., and J. J. Gross. 2010. "Effects of Mindfulness-Based Stress Reduction (MBSR) on Emotion Regulation in Social Anxiety Disorder." *Emotion* 10(1): 83–91.

Hallis, L., L. Cameli, F. Dionne, and B. Knäuper. 2016. "Combining Cognitive Therapy with Acceptance and Commitment Therapy for Depression: A Manualized Group Therapy." *Journal of Psychotherapy Integration* 26(2): 186–201.

Hannah, S. T., P. J. Sweeney, and P. B. Lester. 2010. "The Courageous Mind-Set: A Dynamic Personality System Approach to Courage." In *The Psychology of Courage: Modern Research on an Ancient Virtue,* edited by C. L. S. Pury and S. J. Lopez, 125–148. Washington, DC: American Psychological Association.

Hayes, S. C. 2005. *Get Out of Your Mind and Into Your Life: The New Acceptance and Commitment Therapy.* Oakland, CA: New Harbinger Publications.

Huber, C. 2001. *There Is Nothing Wrong With You.* Rev. ed. Murphys, CA: Keep It Simple Books.

Kabat-Zinn, J., A. O. Massion, J. Kristeller, L. G. Peterson, K. E. Fletcher, L. Pbert, W. R. Lenderking, and S.F. Santorelli.

1992. "Effectiveness of a Meditation-Based Stress Reduction Program in the Treatment of Anxiety Disorders." *American Journal of Psychiatry* 149(7): 936–943.

Lerner, H. 2014. *The Dance of Anger: A Woman's Guide to Changing the Patterns of Intimate Relationships.* New York: William Morrow.

Mascaro, J. S., A. Darcher, L. T. Negi, and C. L. Raison. 2015. "The Neural Mediators of Kindness-Based Meditation: A Theoretical Model." *Frontiers in Psychology* 6: 109. Retrieved from https://www.ncbi.nlm.nih.gov/pmc/articles/PMC4325657.

Mohr, T. S. 2015. *Playing Big: Practical Advice for Women Who Want to Speak Up, Create, and Lead.* New York: Avery.

Mullan, B., V. Allom, and E. Mergelsberg. 2016. "Forming a Habit in a Novel Behavior: The Role of Cues to Action and Self-Monitoring." *EHP: Bulletin of the European Health Psychology Society* 18: 686.

Nelson, S. 2013. *Friendships Don't Just Happen.* Nashville, TN: Turner.

Pury, C. L. S., and S. J. Lopez. 2010. *The Psychology of Courage: Modern Research on an Ancient Virtue.* Washington, DC: American Psychological Association.

Rodriguez, T. 2016. "Study Links 'Neuroflexibility' of Ventromedial Prefrontal Cortex with Stress Resilience." *Psychiarty Advisor.* August 2. http://www.psychiatryadvisor.com/anxiety/positive -health-outcomes-seen-with-active-coping-strategies/article /513438.

Reuell, P. 2015. "How the Brain Builds New Thoughts." *Harvard Gazette*. Retrieved from http://news.harvard.edu/gazette/story /2015/10/how-the-brain-builds-new-thoughts.

Schiller, D. 2010. "Snakes in the MRI Machine: A Study of Courage." *Scientific American*. July 20. https://www.scientific american.com/article/snakes-in-the-mri-machine.

Scott, W., K. E. J. Hann, and L. M. McCracken. 2016. "A Comprehensive Examination of Changes in Psychological Flexibility Following Acceptance and Commitment Therapy for Chronic Pain." *Journal of Contemporary Psychotherapy* 46: 139–148.

Swaminathan, N. 2007. "The Fear Factor: When the Brain Decides It's Time to Scram." *Scientific American*. August 23. https://www.scientificamerican.com/article/the-brain -fear-factor.

Tessler, B. 2016. *The Art of Money: A Life-Changing Guide to Financial Happines*. Berkeley, CA: Parallax Press.

University College London. 2009. "How Long Does It Take to Form a Habit?" August 4. https://www.ucl.ac.uk/news/news -articles/0908/09080401.

Vanzant, I. 2001. *Yesterday, I Cried: Celebrating the Lessons of Living and Loving*. New York: Fireside.

Yin, H. H., and B. J. Knowlton. 2006. "The Role of the Basal Ganglia in Habit Formation." *Nature Reviews Neuroscience* 7(6): 464–476.

Reader Questions and Book Club Guide

Courage Habit book clubs are a great way to work with the material with other like-minded people in your area or to bring the ideas of the Courage Habit into your workplace. To find a group near you, head to https://www.yourcourageouslife.com/courage -habit to find information about others in your area who are using this work. The following questions can help to direct discussion.

Introduction

1. What did you relate to in Kate's Story of how she had been living in a certain way for years, pushing her fears about change away and not even realizing it? How do you tend to handle fear or self-doubt when it comes up for you? Do you tend to push it away, reason past it, or tell it to go away while you push through?

2. Kate shares that no one is "fearless" and that we can't just brush fear to the side. Do you agree or disagree? Why?

3. Habits comprise a cue (such as feeling fear), a routine (a response to that cue), and a reward (some kind of relaxation that comes from going into known and familiar routines). What are some scenarios that cue fear for you?

4. Do you dislike the word "fear"? Do you prefer to call it something else, such as self-doubt, anxiety, nervousness, or a lack of confidence? If so, why? How does calling it something different change the experience of it?

Chapter 1

1. After completing your own "Liberated Day" exercise and identifying your Primary Focus, share the Primary Focus with your reading group. Notice if you feel any fear about sharing or self-doubt about making the necessary changes to bring that most courageous self into your life. Share what you notice.

2. As you listen to others share their "Liberated Day" or Primary Focus, what are some of the ways that the value of courage shows up in each person's responses, even when the things that we each desire are very different?

3. Do you find yourself worrying that your "Liberated Day" or Primary Focus isn't realistic or possible? Why? Consider sharing these worries and seeing if others in your group can name specific people they know or public or historical examples of people who have done the things you'd like to do. Those examples are your proof that it is possible.

4. Research indicates that goals that benefit others are both more satisfying to pursue and more likely to succeed. What's your reason for your Primary Focus? If you step into living from your most courageous self, how will that positively impact the world?

Chapter 2

1. Yasmine and Eliana, both profiled in Chapter 2, had experiences of fear that happened in unexpected ways. Because the fear was showing up differently than they'd expected, they didn't always realize in the moment that they were stuck in their fear. Share about a time when you had a similar experience and only in hindsight could see that you had been stuck in fear.

2. After completing the "Clarifying Your Fears" exercise, share your top three fears with the group. Notice who else has your same fears.

3. Everyone exhibits a few qualities from all the fear routines described in this chapter, but usually there's one fear routine that someone predominantly defaults to more than the others. Which fear routine is your predominant routine? Do you also recognize yourself in parts of other fear routines?

Chapter 3

1. Give the rest of your group some context for your past experiences with any kind of body-based work. Do you find accessing the body to be easy, difficult, or something in between? How did you feel about the idea of doing some body-based work prior to this chapter?

2. Try accessing the body with other members of your book club group. I suggest that you first set a timer for one minute and intentionally laugh with your group, then set the timer for another minute and intentionally dance with the group, and then set the timer for three minutes and just quietly breathe together. When you're finished share what you noticed.

3. Are there any strong emotions that you don't want to encounter? What's the worry about feeling them? Share this with your group and then ask other members of your group to share about how they got unstuck from difficult emotional spaces.

Chapter 4

1. Everyone has a Critic, and everyone's Critic sounds different. After completing the exercises in Chapter 4, share with your group what your Critic sounds like. Everyone in the group can prepare to offer silent but real support in the form of eye contact and holding up what we call in our trainings "the love sign" (the sign language for "love"). To make it with your hand, extend your thumb, index finger, and pinkie finger, while folding down your middle and ring fingers. Then, hold your hand out in this way, with the palm facing out. It's a silent and supportive way to let someone know that you are listening when he or she shares something vulnerable.

2. Would you say you are someone who avoids, pleases, or attacks your Inner Critic voices?

3. Kate shares that when her coach, Matthew, suggested she think of her Critic as her "best friend with lousy communication skills," she was repulsed because she was convinced the Critic couldn't have any good intentions. As she thought about it more, she started to see how in its own dysfunctional way the Critic was trying to criticize her away from taking risks that could result in failures. Consider the Critic voices you shared. Can you see where your Critic might be talking a big game, while really being deeply insecure?

4. Pick one of your Critic's statements and then role-play as your Critic while another member of your circle offers "Re-do, Please" a few times. Share what you notice. As you're doing this, the person who is offering "Re-do, Please" should refrain from giving advice or coaching and just let the person role-playing as the Critic to notice what she experiences. If you're role-playing as your Critic, remember to take a breath after you finish and to reconnect with the group to mentally exit from the role-play experience.

Chapter 5

1. In Chapter 5, Kate shares about how she didn't think she was capable of completing a triathlon because she "just wasn't an athlete." The voice that came up didn't sound critical, but rather it was more matter-of-fact. Is there anything you've ever been interested in doing but assumed that you "just weren't that type of person"? What about your assumptions about "courageous people"? Do you assume that there are some people who are just naturally more courageous and others who aren't?

2. Carolyn had Stories that were influenced by her fear routine (Saboteur). What's your fear routine? What Stories or assumptions tend to go with that routine?

3. After completing the "Identifying Your Stories" and "Common Stories of Limitation" sections of this chapter, share some of your Stories with the group. I suggest that everyone gather in a circle to share what their Stories are without commentary from the group until everyone has shared. You'll likely see that you have at least a few Stories in common. It's a powerful

experience to see how everyone is alike when it comes to making assumptions about how the world works. Are there any Stories of limitation that everyone seems to have in common?

4. Reframing Stories isn't the same as using positive affirmations. Are you a fan of positive affirmations? Why or why not? Share with the group.

5. While you'll come up with your own ideas for reframing your Stories, it can also be interesting to see what a group of people helping you brainstorm can come up with. Have each person in the group share a one-sentence Story, then have the group offer potential reframes. The listener should take care to take away what she feels is helpful and leave the rest. In other words, try not to take it personally if the reframes suggested don't feel like a fit. This group practice can be a great way of identifying any Stories you might have about support in your life (or lack thereof). Do you fully receive or do you dismiss people's suggestions for reframes?

Chapter 6

1. When Kate ran her first course, she was critical of herself and afraid of how others might judge her because participants didn't engage in the way that she'd expected. Kate's friend McCabe gave her an entirely different perspective that allowed Kate to see how fear had been operating without conscious awareness. Kate then realized that reaching out and creating community is important to help us recognize fear routines at work. What or who are the support systems and people in your life that are also engaged in this work?

2. Kate shares the qualities that are practiced in courage-based relationships. Consider the people you interact with most. Do you practice some or all of these qualities? If not, why not? What's the feeling of limitation in that relationship? Share how you have been practicing the behaviors that show up in courage-based relationships. For example, maybe you've always noticed that one person listens deeply or offers empathy when another person struggles by saying, "Me, too."

3. In the "Your Stories About Connection" section, Kate shares many of the common reasons people give for not forming closer relationships. Which of these do you relate to? Have you had any relationships in which you resisted getting closer due to any of these reasons, and then you took the risk and it turned out well?

4. Kate included the section "Difficult Relationships" in this chapter because so many of her clients have shared longings to be more courageous, but they fear that their desires wouldn't be met with support or would be laughed at or criticized. How have you handled comments about how you've changed, criticisms, or judgments from other people? When you read the list of "hiding out" behaviors, which ones are you most likely to default to? Share this with your group. If you are so inclined, you might also ask others in the group to be "accountability partners" around those "hiding out" behaviors. Check in with each other every so often to stay accountable around practicing courage-based behaviors, rather than "hiding out" behaviors.

5. In the "Creating the Ripple Effect" section, examples are given of people who have used the Courage Habit steps not just in their own lives but in their marriages, as parents, or in

their jobs. What are the other domains of your life in which these courageous habits would be useful? What are some action steps you can take to start practicing the Courage Habit in those areas?

Chapter 7

1. It's common for people to want to arrive at a finishing point with personal work and never encounter the same doubt or fears again. Kate suggests seeing your work as part of a process that is ongoing, and trusting the process. Where is it easier for you to trust the process of change? Where does it tend to be harder?

2. As a group, choose three to five different reflection questions that you can each share with the entire group. Highlight at least one way that you have shifted, changed, or grown, even if you feel like there's more to be done. After each individual share, the rest of the group can offer validation, encouragement, and celebration, because every single shift is a worthy one!

3. One of the most difficult aspects of doing group work is figuring out how to handle ending the group and deciding how it will shift and grow from there. What do the group members want to do to keep the good work flowing? After all, you can always choose a new Primary Focus and begin the work of the Courage Habit anew. Is there some kind of accountability or check-in system you'd like to set up? Even if you don't continue with regular book club meetings, consider finding some way, even if it's just an occasional email, to say hello to one another and reconnect.

Kate Swoboda, aka "Kate Courageous," is creator of YourCourageousLife.com, and director of the Courageous Living Coach Certification program. She has been deemed one of the top fifty bloggers in health, fitness, and happiness by Greatist. com. Swoboda has contributed to *Entrepreneur*, Dr. Oz's *The Good Life*, *Forbes*, *USA Today*, *The Intelligent Optimist*, *Lifetime Moms*, *MindBodyGreen*, *Business Insider*, and more, and has spoken about creating better habits and the principles of *The Courage Habit* to groups both large and small. Learn more at www.yourcourageous life.com and www.tribeclcc.com

Foreword writer **Bari Tessler** is a financial therapist and mentor coach. She has guided thousands of people to new, empowered, and refreshingly honest relationships with money through her nurturing, body-centered approach. Tessler is currently leading a global conscious money movement via the year-long program The Art of Money, which she founded in 2001, weaving together money teachings for individuals, couples, and entrepreneurs. She is author of *The Art of Money*.

MORE BOOKS *from*
NEW HARBINGER PUBLICATIONS

Register your **new harbinger** titles for additional benefits!

When you register your **new harbinger** title—purchased in any format, from any source—you get access to benefits like the following:

- Downloadable accessories like printable worksheets and extra content

- Instructional videos and audio files

- Information about updates, corrections, and new editions

Not every title has accessories, but we're adding new material all the time.

Access free accessories in 3 easy steps:

1. Sign in at NewHarbinger.com (or **register** to create an account).

2. Click on **register a book**. Search for your title and click the **register** button when it appears.

3. Click on the **book cover or title** to go to its details page. Click on **accessories** to view and access files.

That's all there is to it!

If you need help, visit:

NewHarbinger.com/accessories

new harbinger
CELEBRATING
40 YEARS